Secret Power
to Faith, Family,
and Getting a Guy

A Personal Bible Study on the Book of Ruth

Susie Shellenberger

ZONDERVAN®

GRAND RAPIDS, MICHIGAN 49530

ZONDERVAN.COM/
AUTHORTRACKER

www.invertbooks.com

Youth Specialties products, 300 South Pierce Street, El Cajon, CA 92020 are published by Zondervan, 5300 Patterson Avenue Southeast, Grand Rapids, MI 49530.

Library of Congress Cataloging-in-Publication Data
Shellenberger, Susie.
  Secret power to faith, family, and getting a guy : a personal Bible study on the book of Ruth / by Susie Shellenberger.
      p. cm.
  ISBN-10: 0-310-25677-1 (pbk.)
  ISBN-13: 978-0-310-25677-9 (pbk.)
  1. Bible. O.T. Ruth—Criticism, interpretation, etc. I. Title.
  BS1315.52.S54 2006
  222'.3500712—dc22

                                                                2006001046

Web site addresses listed in this book were current at the time of publication. Please contact Youth Specialties via e-mail (YS@YouthSpecialties.com) to report URLs that are no longer operational and replacement URLs if available.

Creative Team: Will Penner, Heather Haggerty, and SharpSeven Design
Cover design by Burnkit

Printed in the United States

06 07 08 09 10 11 12 • 10 9 8 7 6 5 4 3 2 1

Table of Contents

Introduction

READ THIS FIRST!

Jacki's parents had decided to get a divorce. Even though she had pleaded with them to try and make it work one more time, their decision was final.

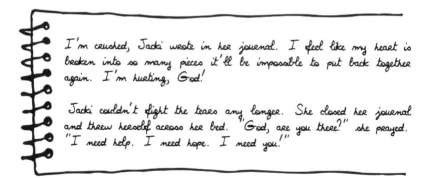

I'm crushed, Jacki wrote in her journal. I feel like my heart is broken into so many pieces it'll be impossible to put back together again. I'm hurting, God!

Jacki couldn't fight the tears any longer. She closed her journal and threw herself across her bed. "God, are you there?" she prayed. "I need help. I need hope. I need you!"

Have you ever felt this way? Has the world ever caved in on you? Whether or not you can identify with Jacki's family situation, I bet you can understand feelings of confusion and despair.

Guess what! The book of Ruth is a book of hope. It proves that God wants to make beautiful things happen through devastating circumstances. Only *God* can take a life full of doubts, questions, and hopelessness and transform it into a life full of promise, love, and purpose. That's what God did for Ruth. And that's exactly what God wants to do for *you* too!

A Move, Two Weddings, Three Funerals, & Another Move

RUTH

Where is it? Ruth is the eighth book in the Old Testament. You can find it between Judges and 1 Samuel. It's a tiny book with only 85 verses, but it's packed with a powerful message that ministers to everyone who feels left out, hopeless, or looking for love.

Who wrote it? Lots of people think Samuel wrote it, but there are hints that Ruth was written after Samuel died. So we're not actually sure who the author is.

To whom is this letter written? It was specifically written to the people of Israel. But we can also say it was written to us because everything in the Bible is relevant forever.

The scene: This book was written during a dark and evil time in the history of Israel. Most people didn't care about pleasing God; they were only interested in themselves. Sound like today's news?

Sounds kinda like: a Cinderella story. One of the main characters—Ruth—goes from poverty to great wealth, from great sadness as a widow to great delight as the wife of an incredibly wonderful man.

BITE #1

In the days when the judges ruled, there was a famine in the land, and a man from Bethlehem in Judah, together with his wife and two sons, went to live for a while in the country of Moab. (Ruth 1:1)

Israel had no kings at this point in its history. Judges ruled the nation. Before we go any further with this verse, let's take a step backward to the book in the Old Testament before Ruth. That book is Judges. It ends with some of the most horrific scenes in the Bible. Why? Because people were only interested in themselves.

Let's take a look at Judges 17:6: "In those days Israel had no king; everyone did as he saw fit."

What's the problem with doing whatever we want?

trouble   craziness

You can imagine the chaotic conditions that permeated Israel during a time of everyone doing his or her own thing! Some Bible commentators have called the last few chapters of Judges "the sewage of Scripture." This section of the Bible contains physical mutilation, rape, murder, and other horrendous acts.

But interestingly, immediately following the book of Judges, we find the book of Ruth—filled with hope and promise. What a stark contrast to what Israel had been experiencing. As Christians we need to remember that even in the darkest days, God can provide hope and healing.

Describe a time when you were in the midst of dark days yet experienced God's hope, healing, and promise.

Katrina/moving to Memphis

> The man's name was Elimelech, his wife's name Naomi, and the
> names of his two sons were Mahlon and Kilion. They were Eph-
> rathites from Bethlehem, Judah. And they went to Moab and lived
> there. (Ruth 1:2)

We're told this family is Ephrathite. *Ephrath* is a word often linked with Bethlehem. Places where *Ephrath* is used throughout the Bible suggest there was an importance, or a special dignity, to being an Ephrathite. Because it's used to describe this particular family, they may have been a well-established family. Perhaps the family was wealthy or held prestige among their neighbors.

This verse also talks about a move. Have you ever moved to a new city?

 _____ Yes

_____ No

If so, what was the most difficult part of your transition?

making friends

Think about the transition you experience when you begin a new school year. You enter new classes and encounter new subjects. What's the toughest part of this transition?

you feel completely lost

BITE #2

Let's think about the Ephrathites' move for a moment—where they're from and where they're going. They're living in the country of Judah, in the city of Bethlehem. *Bethlehem* means "house of bread," and it's the city where Jesus would be born centuries later.

Choose the letter that best describes the connection between Jesus and "house of bread."

_____ a.   Bethlehem is the "house of bread," and Jesus lived on bread alone.
_____ b.   Jesus ate only bread for the first five years of his life.
___✓___ c.   Bethlehem is the "house of bread," and Jesus is the Bread of Life.
_____ d.   Jesus ate a lot of raisin bread.

Judah means "praise." So this family is living in the city of **bread** in the midst of *praise.* Sounds like a great place! And we can assume the family described in Ruth 1:2 is happy. Take a look at their names and what their names mean:

Elimelech: "God is my King."

Naomi: "Pleasant."

How does your name describe **you?**

Rachel – gentle, innocent, blessed one

Why would a happy family choose to leave such a **great** place and journey to Moab?

They left Bethlehem, Judah, when a **famine** hit the land. *But how could a famine hit such a wonderful place,* you may be thinking, *a place filled with praise for God?*

Let's take a quick peek at 2 Chronicles 7:19-20.

> But if you turn away and forsake the decrees and commands I have given you and go off to serve other gods and worship them, then I will uproot Israel from my land, which I have given them, and will reject this temple I have consecrated for my Name.

In this passage we learn that if people turn away from God,

___✓___ **a.**   God may take the Israelites' land away or force them to move.
_____ b.   God probably won't notice.
_____ c.   They'll never eat bread again.
_____ **d.**   They'll only have bread to eat the rest of their lives.

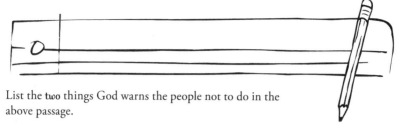

List the two things God warns the people not to do in the above passage.

1. worship false gods
2. don't follow his commands

What does it mean to serve other gods?

 worship them

List some idols that Christians often let slip into their lives.

famous people

Let's also look at 2 Chronicles 7:14.

> If my people, who are called by my name, will humble themselves and pray and seek my face and turn from their wicked ways, then will I hear from heaven and will forgive their sin and will heal their land.

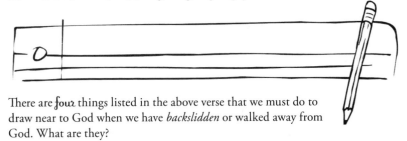

There are *four* things listed in the above verse that we must do to draw near to God when we have *backslidden* or walked away from God. What are they?

1. turn from wicked ways
2. humble ourselves
3. pray
4. seek God

And what is the promise when we come back to God?

forgive our sin & heal our land

BITE #3

Back to the story in Ruth. Evidently people in the city of bread and the place of praise are turning away from God. It may have been in subtle ways at first, but there *is* a turning away from God. The result?

_____ a.   No more popcorn.
_____ b.   Schools closed.
_____ c.   Shopping malls went under.
___✓___ d.   Famine.

Whenever we turn away from God, we can always expect a *famine*—dry times. We can expect to experience a famine when God doesn't have the proper place in our lives. But there is more than one kind of famine.

Check out Amos 8:11:

> "The days are coming," declares the Sovereign LORD, "when I will send a famine through the land—not a famine of food or a thirst for water, but a famine of hearing the words of the Lord."

Can you relate to this kind of famine? Identify a time in your life when you felt like you weren't hearing from God—a time when God felt distant.

Katrina & the move

All of us will experience times of spiritual famine. The issue becomes: What will you do when spiritually dry times hit? We learn from 2 Chronicles that the cure for famine is to wait where you are and call on God. This is where many people jump the gun. Instead of humbling themselves, calling on God, and waiting for God's response and direction, they immediately seek a fast-food buffet of spiritual excitement.

They become church hoppers, or they float from one set of friends to another, or they read a variety of spiritual books—when they should simply keep reading the Bible, continue calling on God for help, and wait for God's guidance.

Instead of waiting out the famine, Elimelech and his family move to Moab. Grab your Bible and flip to Psalm 108:9. How is Moab described?

a safe God-protected place

God's bathtub

Think about this picture: A godly family leaves the city of bread and the place of praise and moves to a garbage dump, a washbasin. What other Bible story reminds you of this?

_____ a. Jesus heals a blind man.
_____ b. Jesus raises Lazarus from the dead.
___✓___ c. The prodigal son leaves a wonderful home and eats with pigs in a pigpen.
_____ d. Jesus heals a deaf man.

You might consider this the story of a prodigal **family**. When famine hits their land, they leave. Perhaps they get scared and let fear rule their decisions instead of **faith**. This is only one of 13 famines mentioned in the Bible. Each time there's a famine in the Bible, it's presented as a judgment from God.

Elimelech and his family should **trust** God to take care of them. They should wait out the famine, continually humbling themselves before the Lord. But instead they flee to the land of **Moab**.

Identify a time when you should have **trusted** God, but instead you became impatient or frightened and acted on your own without waiting on God.

now when i'm nervous about high school & upset about not haveing a relationship

🍴 BITE #4

> Now Elimelech, Naomi's husband, died, and she was left with her two sons. (Ruth 1:3)

Have you ever lost a loved one through **death?** If yes, describe who died, how it happened, and the hurt you experienced. If not, describe the hurt you felt when someone close to you moved away or left.

Sugar it was sad

Let's keep reading and find out what the sons do after their father dies.

> They married Moabite women, one named Orpah and the other Ruth. (Ruth 1:4)

When Naomi's sons marry Moabite women, they immediately break the Mosaic law—the Old Testament law. They are intermingling with a foreign people, and God had warned them against doing so (Numbers 36).

Look at the *downhill progression* of this family. It starts with impatience and unwillingness to humble themselves and to seek and wait on the Lord. Then they move against God's will to a place exactly the opposite of being in the city of bread and the house of praise. They move to an *ungodly* environment and set up home.

Remember what Elimelech's name means?

_____ a.   Chocolate cake lover.
___✓___ b.   God is my King.
_____ c.   Marathon runner.
_____ d.   God scares me.

It's extremely tough to live out *"God is my King"* in an ungodly environment where we can't surround ourselves with godly people and enter into God's house of praise. Elimelech has moved his family to the *garbage dump* of cities.

Life has become extremely difficult; Elimelech dies. And probably because he has taken his sons away from the house of praise, God's *laws* aren't as important to them anymore. They aren't **connected** with other believers. Their *morals* have slipped, and they break the Old Testament law by **compromising** and marrying women who worship foreign gods.

What does it mean to **compromise**?

to trade on thing for another

Describe a time in your life when **you** compromised.

I said I would moved if I got my own room & $cat₊ tv

What were the consequences?

good things

What things tempt us to compromise our relationship with Christ? Circle all that apply and list others that come to your mind.

peer
chocolate chip cookies
God's love
non-Christian friends
wanting our own way
fear
pressure
secrets
temptation
impatience
lust
God's direction
rumors
seeking
selfish desires
reading the Bible
skipping church
faith
memorizing Scripture
a strong prayer life
other: _____

Sometimes we're tempted to think we can hide our compromises from God. But the Bible tells us God sees and knows everything. Grab your Bible and turn to Hebrews 4:13 and paraphrase (rewrite) this passage in your own words:

Write a prayer in the space below telling God you don't want to compromise. Ask God to help you stand firm during tough times and not give in to the temptation to compromise.

BITE #5

> After they had lived there about ten years, both Mahlon and
> Kilion also died, and Naomi was left without her two sons and her
> husband. (Ruth 1:4-5)

Ten years pass. Naomi may feel as though she's lost everything. If we don't keep God in the *priority* position in our lives, when tough times come, it's easy to feel as if we've lost everything. It's easy to get *discouraged*. Naomi still has her faith in God; she simply needs to activate it and recharge her relationship with God.

When you realize you're not where you should be spiritually, what should you do to *recharge* your relationship with Christ? (There are actually four things you should do, and you can get the answers from recapping 2 Chronicles 7:14, Bite #2.)

1.

2.

3.

4.

> When she heard in Moab that the Lord had come to the aid of his
> people by providing food for them, Naomi and her daughters-in-
> law prepared to return home from there. (Ruth 1:6)

The famine has *ended* in Bethlehem. The city of bread is filled with praise once again, and Naomi wants to *return* where she knows she should have been all along—in the city of Bethlehem in the country of Judah.

Mark your three favorite bread items:

_____	wheat bread	_____	cinnamon bread
_____	white bread	_____	gingerbread
_____	sourdough bread	_____	rye bread
_____	raisin bread	_____	French bread
_____	bread pudding	_____	garlic bread
_____	homemade bread	_____	multigrain bread

Naomi remembers what life had been like in the city of bread and the house of praise. No doubt she has kept those memories alive in her mind and often turned to them during times of grief and depression.

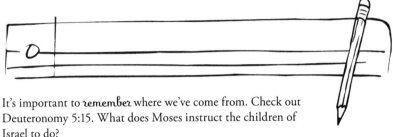

It's important to *remember* where we've come from. Check out Deuteronomy 5:15. What does Moses instruct the children of Israel to do?

Now flip over to Deuteronomy 8:2. What does Moses instruct the children of Israel to do?

Now turn back to Exodus 13:3. What is Moses asking the people to remember?

Take a moment to **remember** your life before you met Christ and sought forgiveness for your sins. What's the biggest *difference* in your life now versus then?

BITE #6

With her two daughters-in-law she left the place where she had been living and set out on the road that would take them back to the land of Judah. (Ruth 1:7)

Naomi is headed home. We can only imagine the excitement and peace she feels as she pursues the road that will lead her to where she knows God wants her to be.

Think of a time when you were away from home for a while. Perhaps it was camp, a mission trip, or a visit to relatives. How did it feel when you finally got back to your home?

What three things do you miss most when you're away from your home?

1.

2.

3.

Then Naomi said to her two daughters-in-law, "Go back, each of you, to your mother's home. May the Lord show kindness to you, as you have shown to your dead and to me. May the Lord grant that each of you will find rest in the home of another husband." (Ruth 1:8-9)

Naomi isn't bitter. No doubt she has grieved the death of her husband and her two sons, but it's clear that she wants the best for her two daughters-in-law.

Then she kissed them and they wept aloud and said to her, "We will go back with you to your people." (Ruth 1:9-10)

The above verse indicates they have been a close family. How would you describe your family?

But Naomi said, "Return home, my daughters. Why would you come with me? Am I going to have any more sons, who could become your husbands? Return home, my daughters; I am too old to have another husband. Even if I thought there was still hope for me—even if I had a husband tonight and gave birth to sons— would you wait until they grew up? Would you remain unmarried for them? No, my daughters. It is more bitter for me than for you, because the Lord's hand has gone out against me!" (Ruth 1:11-13)

This has the makings of a great *chick flick*. It's filled with emotion, honesty, and wonderful dialogue. Naomi is basically telling Ruth and Orpah that she has lost *everything* in Moab. She has nothing, and she'll return to nothing in Bethlehem. Her love for her daughters-in-law (who probably seem like actual daughters to her by now) motivates her to encourage them to seek their own *happiness*.

Naomi knows the problems her girls will face if they return to Bethlehem, Judah, with her. Moabites and Israelites don't have anything to do with one another. Her daughters-in-law will face rejection, gossip, and *hardship* if they return with her to Bethlehem.

Imagine yourself in Ruth's or Orpah's shoes. How would you have responded to Naomi?

It's as if Naomi is saying, "Girls, you won't be able to remarry in Bethlehem. *No one will have you.* You're both young; you should remarry and have your own families. I've lost all my property. Why would you choose to return with me? You'll experience *poverty* and *widowhood* the rest of your life. If you come with me, the cost is high. *It will cost you everything.*"

What's the parallel between what Naomi is telling Ruth and Orpah and what Christ tells us?

_____ a.   If we follow Christ, we can't get married.
_____ b.   If we follow Christ, we have to move to Bethlehem.
_____ c.   If we follow Christ, it will cost us everything.
_____ d.   If we follow Christ, we'll always live in poverty.

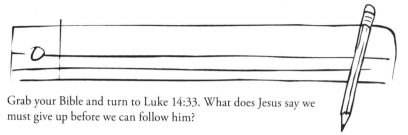

Grab your Bible and turn to Luke 14:33. What does Jesus say we must give up before we can follow him?

Now turn to Matthew 19:27. What does Peter say to Jesus?

And what is Christ's response to Peter in Matthew 19:29? What will we receive in return for following Christ?

Have you given up everything to follow Jesus?

Ask God to reveal any area of your life that you're still clinging to; then ask for the willingness to give that up. Tell God you're willing to empty your life completely and follow Christ with abandon!

BITE #7

At this they wept again. Then Orpah kissed her mother-in-law good-by, but Ruth clung to her. (Ruth 1:14)

Why do you suppose Orpah goes back to Moab?

Orpah's name means "youthful" or "immature." Her reaction is one of an immature believer. No doubt Naomi has not only kept her faith alive during the past 10 years in Moab, but she has also grown in her faith. And her daughters-in-law have witnessed her spiritual growth firsthand. We're led to believe that Ruth and Orpah have grown to love Naomi so much that they have also fallen in love with her God.

But this verse shows us the difference between the two girls' spiritual maturity. Orpah leaves her newfound faith in the true God and returns to idols and false gods in Moab. Ruth, however, refuses to go back. She's making a clean break!

Take another look at Ruth 1:14. What action does Orpah demonstrate with Naomi?

What action does Ruth demonstrate?

Do you see the difference between the two? One is expressing **emotion**; the other is expressing devotion. Which one does Ruth express?

Think about your own relationship with Christ. When you're surrounded by other Christians (church camp, retreats, Bible study, youth group, etc.), it's easy to get caught up in expressing emotion. But eventually you have to come down off the spiritual mountaintop. So what happens when camp is over?

What happens when the emotion is gone, the music has faded, and your friends have gone their separate ways? If your relationship with Christ is based on emotion, it won't last long. But if you've grounded your relationship with Jesus on devotion, it can surely weather the hard times. It will be real and lasting.

Take a moment to evaluate your emotion versus devotion factor. Mark each of the following statements true or false.

————— I tend to express my love for God mostly through emotion.

————— I tend to express my love for God through prayer, Bible reading, and obedience.

————— If I'm not surrounded by other Christians, I often question my faith in God.

————— If I can't feel God, I doubt God's existence.

————— I sometimes feel God's presence, but other times I don't. My faith remains consistent and isn't based on what I feel. I base my relationship with God on fact, not feeling.

————— When God seems far away, I assume God is far away.

————— When God seems far away, I still believe God's with me because of the promise that God will never leave me.

————— My relationship with Christ tends to revolve around my emotions—what I'm feeling and how I'm feeling.

————— My relationship with Christ is based on the fact that I have chosen to follow him whether I feel his presence or not.

What's the difference in demonstrating emotion and demonstrating devotion?

Orpah *kisses* Naomi, but Ruth *clings* to her. Orpah is close to her mother-in-law, but Ruth has become a part of her life. Describe the difference in being close to Christ and actually becoming one with him.

Are you close to Christ—simply living next to him? Or are you attaching yourself to him and enjoying the process of becoming part of him?

BITE #8

"Look," said Naomi, "your sister-in-law is going back to her people and her gods. Go back with her."

But Ruth replied, "Don't urge me to leave you or to turn back from you. Where you go I will go, and where you stay I will stay. Your people will be my people and your God my God." (Ruth 1:15-16)

Ruth has clearly *decided* to forsake all idols and false gods for Naomi's true God. Evidently, she sees so much *fruit* of a growing, active relationship with God in Naomi's life, she can't help but desire the same thing.

What *evidences* of God do you hope people see in **your** life?

Let's look at the *fruit of the Spirit* that God wants to cultivate in every believer's life.

> But the fruit of the Spirit is love, joy, peace, patience, kindness, goodness, faithfulness, gentleness and self-control. (Galatians 5:22-23)

Which of the above are demonstrated in Naomi's life with her daughters-in-law?

Circle the following fruits that are most evident in your life:

gentleness
patience self-faithfulness
love control
joy peace goodness kindness

Circle the following fruits that are least evident in your life:

gentleness
patience self-faithfulness
love control
joy peace goodness kindness

Pause for a moment and ask God to help you cultivate *each* fruit of the Spirit in your life.

> Where you die I will die, and there I will be buried. May the LORD deal with me, be it ever so severely, if anything but death separates you and me. (Ruth 1:17)

What similarities do you see in Ruth's devotion to Naomi and a Christian's devotion to Christ?

BITE #9

Ruth makes a seven-part commitment to Naomi. Complete the statements that show each commitment she makes:

∗ Where you go, _____.

∗ Where you stay, _____.

∗ Your people _____.

∗ Your God _____.

∗ Where you die, _____.

∗ _____ I will be buried.

∗ May the Lord deal with me _____
   if anything but _____ separates
   you and me.

What a commitment! Let's look in turn at each *part* of Ruth's commitment.

#1: When Ruth says she'll go with Naomi, she isn't simply seeking a *passport* out of the garbage dump to the city of bread. When you *first* made a commitment to Christ, it may have been so you could have the assurance of going to *heaven* or escaping *hell*. But as you grow in your relationship with him, you begin to fall in love with Christ. Though you look forward to being with Christ forever in heaven, you also enjoy your relationship with him *right now*.

List three things you love about your relationship with Christ right now:

1.

2.

3.

List three things you're looking forward to experiencing in heaven:

1.

2.

3.

#2: Next Ruth says she'll *stay* with Naomi when they arrive in Bethlehem. In other words Ruth is willing to *identify* with Naomi and her poverty. She isn't planning on forsaking the old woman to seek her own riches. She's not going to Bethlehem, Judah, to chase guys; she's going to be a part of Naomi's *life* and serve Naomi's *God*.

Christ wants you to *identify* with him. If you've completed the *Secret Power for Girls* Bible study of 1 Peter, you already know that we're encouraged to identify with Christ in his *suffering*. In what area of your life are you making an effort to *identify* with your Savior?

#3: Ruth claims that Naomi's *people* will become her own people. She's willing to leave *behind* the friendships and relationships that have kept her from becoming all God wants her to be.

Have you had to give up a friendship or relationship because it was hindering your relationship with Christ? If so, describe that. If not, describe what you think that would be like.

Is there a friendship or relationship you **need** to give up to become all that God wants you to be? If so, describe that.

#4: Ruth also claims that Naomi's God will be her God. She's *forsaking* idols and other gods and those who worship them so she can give her life to God Almighty.

What have you forsaken to follow Christ with all your **life?**

#5: Ruth is determined to *die* in the same land where Naomi will die. This proves Ruth's commitment isn't temporary. She's thinking ahead—even unto death.

When we give Christ our **all,** we die (in a sense) to our rights, our wills, and our own selfish desires. Grab your Bible and turn to Galatians 2:20. What does the apostle Paul claim has happened to him?

Have you truly *died* to your will, your rights, and your desires? A eulogy is the speech given at a funeral when someone dies. Take a moment to write a eulogy for yourself, explaining the areas of your life that you are crucifying on the cross to live fully for Jesus.

BITE #10

#6: Ruth claims she will be *buried* in the place she will die (in Bethlehem, Judah, where Naomi will also die—rather than in Moab, where Ruth is from and would've been buried if she had stayed). How does this prove that her commitment isn't a spur-of-the-moment emotional promise?

How does her intention to be buried where she will die make her commitment genuine?

#7: Ruth is so *serious* about her commitment that she seals it by asking God to deal severely with her if she ever breaks it. How would a similar prayer or covenant change the commitment of many Christians?

Ruth concludes her seven-part pledge to Naomi by telling her that nothing besides *death* will separate her from her mother-in-law.

Many Christians would let a lot *less* than death separate them from God. Many have easily turned their backs on God and given up their faith. List some things people allow to *separate* them from God.

*   *

*   *

*   *

*   *

> When Naomi realized that Ruth was determined to go with her, she stopped urging her. (Ruth 1:18)

Naomi realizes Ruth is extremely *serious* about her commitment to God. What can other people see—proven by your lifestyle—that shows *you're* serious about your commitment to Christ?

> So the two women went on until they came to Bethlehem. When they arrived in Bethlehem, the whole town was stirred because of them, and the women exclaimed, "Can this be Naomi?" (Ruth 1:19)

Finally! The prodigal family returns home to Bethlehem. But it's not an entire family any longer; it's simply Naomi and Ruth. It has been 10 years since Naomi's friends have seen her. Imagine the excitement at this *reunion*!

Think of a time you were *away* from home for a while and describe what your *return* was like.

BITE #11

> "Don't call me Naomi," she told them. "Call me Mara, because the Almighty has made my life very bitter. I went away full, but the LORD has brought me back empty. Why call me Naomi? The LORD has afflicted me; the Almighty has brought misfortune upon me." (Ruth 1:20-21)

Remember—Naomi's name means *"pleasant."* She left Bethlehem with a husband and two sons. She had a *full* life. But she has returned a widow with a foreign daughter-in-law who is also a widow. It's obvious that Naomi has *suffered* a great deal in the past 10 years.

But when we **choose** to leave the city of bread and the house of praise—when we choose to walk away from where God has placed us—we should *expect* rough times. The Bible is clear that God will *discipline* us when needed.

What's the advantage of being disciplined?

When someone disciplines me, what does it prove?

_____ a.   That person hates me.

_____ b.   That person loves me enough to help me see what I did was wrong and is willing to help me correct it.

_____ c.   I never really was a Christian.

_____ d.   I can't do anything right.

Let's check out Hebrews 12:5-6:

> And you have forgotten that word of encouragement that addresses you as sons: "My son, do not make light of the Lord's discipline, and do not lose heart when he rebukes you, because the Lord disciplines those he loves, and he punishes everyone he accepts as a son."

According to the above passage, what two things is God proving to you when he disciplines you?

1.

2.

Now let's look at Hebrews 12:7:

> Endure hardship as discipline; God is treating you as sons. For what son is not disciplined by his father?

According to the above verse, how should Naomi view her hardship?

Now read Hebrews 12:10.

> Our fathers disciplined us for a little while as they thought best;
> but God disciplines us for our good, that we may share in his
> holiness.

According to this verse, God disciplines us for which two reasons?

1.

2.

Now grab your Bible and read Hebrews 12:11. What two things will result from God's discipline on our lives?

1.

2.

Back to Naomi. She tells her friends to call her Mara—which means sad or gloomy. You'd think her friends would see her plight and do what she suggests—call her Mara. But they don't. Check out the last verse in chapter one:

> So Naomi returned from Moab accompanied by Ruth the Moabi-
> tess, her daughter-in-law, arriving in Bethlehem as the barley
> harvest was beginning. (Ruth 1:22)

Who returns? **Naomi.** Her friends refuse to let Naomi's situation label her lifestyle.

Because her friends have strong relationships with God, they see the same potential in Naomi that God sees—promise, hope, and fulfillment.

When **you've** been disciplined, experienced rough times, and feel empty, you may be tempted to allow your actions to reflect your feelings. Don't! Jesus always sees your potential. Christ focuses on what you can become with his help. And he wants you to focus on his restoration in your life as well!

Describe a time in your life when you felt *discouraged* and empty yet someone else was able to help you focus on the *bright* side.

BITE #12

GRAB A FRIEND.

Congrats! You made it through the first chapter of Ruth. Now grab a friend and discuss the following questions together.

✳ In the first bite we looked at Judges 17:6: "In those days Israel had no king; everyone did as he saw fit." Has there been a time this past week when I wanted my own way but did what was right instead?

✳ What have I done this past week to ensure I don't experience a spiritual famine?

✳ Is there any area of my life in which I compromised this week?

✳ How have I shown the fruit of the Spirit in my life this week?

MEMORIZE IT!

Try to memorize this verse with your friend and say it to each other the next time you get together.

> "Where you go I will go, and where you stay I will stay. Your people will be my people and your God my God. Where you die I will die, and there I will be buried." (Ruth 1:16-17)

MY JOURNAL

Okay, S.P.G. (Secret Power Girl). This is your space, so take advantage of it. You can do whatever you want with this space but always try to include the following:

* List your prayer requests. (Later, as God answers them, go back and record the dates when God answered your prayers.)

* Copy down any verse we studied in the previous chapter that you don't understand. Then let this be a reminder to ask your parents, Sunday school teacher, pastor, or youth leader about it.

* Jot down what stood out most to you from this chapter.

Girl Meets Guy

BITE #1

Now Naomi had a relative on her husband's side, from the clan of
Elimelech, a man of standing, whose name was Boaz. And Ruth
the Moabitess said to Naomi, "Let me go to the fields and pick
up the leftover grain behind anyone in whose eyes I find favor."
(Ruth 2:1-2)

We get some important information in this first verse. As readers we're being let
in on a **secret**. Most books don't reveal their secrets until the last chapter, but here
we learn that Boaz is a relative—a kinsman—of Naomi. That will take on great
significance in this book—in fact, the rest of the story will revolve around this
secret—but we'll save that for later.

The name Boaz means "standing in strength." He's an impressive man with an
important heritage. He comes from the tribe of Judah. From Boaz would come David,
and eventually the King of Kings (Jesus Christ) would come from this same line.

Grab your Bible and turn to 1 Kings 7:21. Read this passage to find out what
David's son Solomon names after his impressive great-great-grandfather, Boaz.

If you could designate something to be named after **you,** what would you select and why? (Try to think of something that will reflect your personality or your character.)

We also learn from this passage that Ruth doesn't tag along with Naomi, expecting her mother-in-law to provide for her. She's not along for a free ride. She's willing to work. This speaks highly of Ruth's character.

Think about your own character for a moment. If an adult outside your family (pastor, youth leader, school teacher, etc.) were asked to describe your character, what would he or she say?

Naomi said to her, "Go ahead, my daughter." So she went out and began to glean in the fields behind the harvesters. (Ruth 2:2-3)

The gleaning issue was part of a strange law. It's mentioned in Leviticus 19:9-10.

> When you reap the harvest of your land, do not reap to the very edges of your field or gather the gleanings of your harvest. Do not go over your vineyard a second time or pick up the grapes that have fallen. Leave them for the poor and the alien. I am the LORD your God.

This was God's way of telling the Israelites they had to take care of the poor and those from other countries. There was no welfare; food stamps weren't available; and there were no soup kitchens. So the poor were taken care of in this unusual way.

They had to glean—or work for the grain—but it was free to them. This strange law is directed to the landowners and is stated again in Leviticus 23:22:

> When you reap the harvest of your land, do not reap to the very edges of your field or gather the gleanings of your harvest. Leave them for the poor and the alien. I am the LORD your God.

Now grab your Bible and turn to Deuteronomy 24:19. According to this passage, what are the harvesters **not** to do?

This was God's wonderful way of caring for the needy. Instead of lining them up for charity or putting them in a bread line, God put them to work. Machines weren't available in those days, and gleaning by hand was extremely hard work. When the harvesters gleaned by hand, they left approximately 30 percent of the grain in the field. They simply couldn't get it all. And once they'd gone through the field, God told them **not** to go back and pick up the leftovers; these were to be left for the poor.

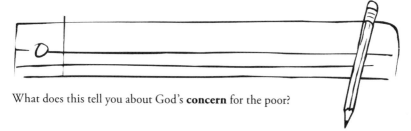

What does this tell you about God's **concern** for the poor?

Now that you understand a little more about the gleaning process, what does this tell you about Ruth's work ethic?

What are **you** doing to help the needy?

List some things you and your friends could do to help the less fortunate. (Could you tutor a child, serve in a soup kitchen, sponsor a child through Compassion International, etc.?)

BITE #2

As it turned out, she found herself working in a field belonging to Boaz, who was from the clan of Elimelech. (Ruth 2:3)

It's obvious that Ruth's priorities are right. She's not chasing guys (though she certainly could be; she's single and young, and it would be much easier to be taken care of than to have to take care of herself and her mother-in-law). She's not in the fields to find someone she can meet. Ruth is working hard, and she's doing backbreaking labor.

Instead of hoping God will plop food in her lap, she takes the initiative. Is there something in your life you've been waiting on God for? It could be that God's waiting on **you** to take the initiative.

According Ruth 2:3, to whom is Boaz related?

And do you remember the relation of Elimelech to Naomi?

_____ a.   He is Naomi's third cousin on her great-aunt's side.
_____ b.   He is Naomi's servant.
_____ c.   He is Naomi's brother.
_____ d.   He is Naomi's husband.

Now it's time to take a look at the special kinsman-redeemer law. This was another strange law God set into place to help his people.

This kinsman-redeemer law is outlined in Leviticus 25. Here's how the law worked: God had told the people of Israel they would enter the Promised Land and could claim that land for themselves. But they could keep the land only as long as they were faithful to God. When they were unfaithful to God, he would put them out of the land.

God placed them in the land according to tribes. A specific tribe had a certain section of the land. Then it was broken down further: Each family within each tribe got a particular plot of land.

So let's imagine Mr. Smith owns 40 acres of land that has been designated to him and his family. Let's also imagine that Mr. Smith has three years of little rain and poor crops, and as a result, he's in desperate need of **money**. What's he going to do?

Here's where another strange law comes into play: the Year of Jubilee.

Let's say Mr. Smith has a rich neighbor. We'll call him Mr. Jones. He sees the opportunity to make some money. Mr. Jones decides to take a mortgage on Mr. Smith's land. But here's where it gets interesting. Mr. Jones can only take up to a **50-year** mortgage because during the Year of Jubilee every mortgage is canceled. The land returns to its original owner.

Strange law, huh? But this law kept land in a family. Still…it's a long wait between jubilees. Mr. Smith might be 60 years old when Mr. Jones offers to take his mortgage. But in 50 years, Mr. Smith will probably be dead. So he won't profit from it. But because the land will stay in the Smith family, the land will go to Mr. Smith's son in 50 years.

Let's make this scenario a little more complicated. Let's assume that Mr. Jones mortgaged the Smith property for 50 years. But five years into this process, Mr. Smith's **wealthy uncle** (his kinsman) moves to town. He can pay the mortgage off and restore the land to Mr. Smith, redeeming him from the mortgage. This way Mr. Smith won't have to wait 45 more years until the Year of Jubilee.

It would be terrific to have a rich uncle as a redeemer, wouldn't it? The kinsman-redeemer is a wonderful picture of our Lord Jesus Christ. He is our kinsman-redeemer. And he's the reason the word *redemption* is used in the New Testament instead of *atonement*.

Atonement simply covered up sins—that's all. But redemption means to pay a price so that the one who's been redeemed is able to go free! Jesus Christ not only died to redeem people, but he also died to redeem the earth. We live on an earth that will someday be delivered from the bondage of corruption. There will be a new heaven and a new earth; that's part of God's redemption plan, as well as redeeming people. God has a perfect and wonderful way of caring for people and creation.

Boaz is related to Naomi's deceased husband, Elimelech. So Boaz will get a chance to become a kinsman-redeemer to Ruth. But we're getting ahead of ourselves. Let's slow down, back up, and keep diving into the Scriptures. We'll eventually come to the plot in this **romance** where the kinsman-redeemer starts to look like a hero!

> Just then Boaz arrived from Bethlehem and greeted the harvesters, "The Lord be with you!"
>
> "The Lord bless you!" they called back. (Ruth 2:4)

We don't need a zoom lens to get a clear picture of Boaz's character from the above passage. Boaz is the rich guy, the landowner. He hires the harvesters. We could compare him to a company president. It's rare that the president of the organization mixes with the temps. Boaz walks right among the workers.

And God does the same with us. Our rich King—the One who created and controls the entire world—has always walked with people, beginning way back in the Garden of Eden.

Grab your Bible and turn to Genesis 3:8. When did God walk with Adam?

God also walked with people in the nation of Israel. Read Exodus 40:34-38. Where was God's *glory*?

Then God came in the form of a human being and walked among us through the person of Jesus Christ. *Today* God still walks with us through the Holy Spirit that dwells within us. God also walks with us through the *church* (the body of Christ).

Describe three things that make you aware of God's presence.

1.

2.

3.

BITE #3

Boaz asked the foreman of his harvesters, "Whose young woman is that?"

The foreman replied, "She is the Moabitess who came back from Moab with Naomi. She said, 'Please let me glean and gather among the sheaves behind the harvesters.' She went into the field and has worked steadily from morning till now, except for a short rest in the shelter." (Ruth 2:5-7)

It's obvious that *Boaz*

_____ a.   Is hungry.
_____ b.   Is interested in finding out who Ruth is.
_____ c.   Is wishing he had a computer.
_____ d.   Is mentally slow.

People know who *Ruth* is. She stands out in a *good* way. Ruth doesn't simply become part of the *crowd*.

Think about yourself for a moment. Do you

_____ a.   Stand out in a good way?
_____ b.   Simply become part of the crowd?
_____ c.   Stand out in a negative way?

Think of two things you can do to stand out in a positive way.

1.

2.

We also learn from Ruth 2:5-7 that she

_____ a.   Works steadily.
_____ b.   Is a lazy bum.
_____ c.   Desperately wants a cola.
_____ d.   Hates anything made with grain.

Even though the law stated that Ruth was eligible to glean behind the harvesters, she still asks *permission*. What does this tell you about her character?

> So Boaz said to Ruth, "My daughter, listen to me. Don't go and glean in another field and don't go away from here. Stay here with my servant girls." (Ruth 2:8)

Clearly Boaz is going out of his way to make sure Ruth *knows* it's not only okay to glean in his field but he also *wants* her to glean in his field!

Describe a time when someone went out of his or her way to make you feel *welcome*.

Describe a time when you went out of your way to make someone else feel welcome.

> "Watch the field where the men are harvesting, and follow along after the girls. I have told the men not to touch you. And whenever you are thirsty, go and get a drink from the water jars the men have filled." (Ruth 2:9)

Okay, Boaz is no longer simply being courteous. He's actually watching over Ruth. He's taking care of her. He's interested!

Who are the people in your life who try to protect you and take care of you?

Notice Ruth's **response** to Boaz's offer of protection.

> At this, she bowed down with her face to the ground. She exclaimed, "Why have I found such favor in your eyes that you notice me—a foreigner?" (Ruth 2:10)

Ruth isn't flippant in her gratitude. She makes sure there is no doubt in the mind of Boaz that she's extremely appreciative. She knows he's going out of his way. She doesn't deserve such care or provision.

Describe a time when you received undeserved grace.

Ruth certainly didn't expect such a *favorable* response from such an important man as Boaz. Remember—Naomi had warned her that life in Bethlehem wouldn't be easy. That's why Orpah decided not to make the journey. Orpah didn't want to face the hardship and risk of remaining a widow living in *poverty* the rest of her life. So she opted to stay in Moab.

Ruth, however, was willing to make the **sacrifice**. And now God is *blessing* her obedience! Note that Ruth is a foreigner, but Boaz's concern and love for her break through all racial *barriers*.

The Israelites looked *down* on the Moabites. The Moabites, at times, were even shut out from the congregation of the Lord—what we might call "church."

How does Boaz remind you of Christ?

Grab your Bible and read Romans 5:8. According to this verse, *when* did Christ die for you?

And according to our story in Ruth, *when* does Boaz show compassion toward this foreigner Ruth?

_____ a.   When she's dressed in her best and well-groomed.
_____ b.   When she's filthy, sweaty, and tired from working all day.
_____ c.   When she's had a fresh manicure and is wearing new perfume.
_____ d.   When she's had highlights put in her hair.

BITE #4

Boaz replied, "I've been told all about what you have done for your mother-in-law since the death of your husband—how you left your father and mother and your homeland and came to live with a people you did not know before. May the LORD repay you for what you have done. May you be richly rewarded by the LORD, the God of Israel, under whose wings you have come to take refuge." (Ruth 2:11-12)

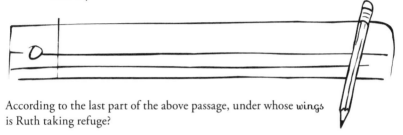

According to the last part of the above passage, under whose wings is Ruth taking refuge?

Perhaps you've heard the phrase, "I want to be the hands and feet of Jesus." Who is being the hands and feet of God in the above passage for Ruth?

When were **you** the hands or feet of Christ to someone?

The first part of this passage informs us that news about Ruth and her wonderful relationship with her mother-in-law has gotten around. People know about her. They're talking about her—and they're saying good things!

We're clearly told in the book of James (4:11) not to *gossip*. Gossip is usually a negative action, and that's what the apostle James warns us against. But here's an example of *positive* gossip! Think of someone you know and list three pieces of positive gossip you can share with others about him or her.

1.

2.

3.

Strive to make it a good habit to *spread* positive gossip about others. God **loves** it when we affirm others and build them up. By spreading positive gossip, you can (mark all that apply)

_____ a.   Start a new trend.
_____ b.   Help someone feel good about himself or herself.
_____ c.   Contribute in a good way to someone's reputation.
_____ d.   Help others have a clearer view of the person about whom you're speaking.

Ruth has placed her faith in Naomi's *God*. Boaz too is a God-fearing man. And now that he's *met* Ruth, he realizes that all the good things he has heard about her are *true*. He's deeply attracted to her, and *romance* is beginning to stir in his heart!

The best kind of relationships are those that are

_____ a.   Based on looks.
_____ b.   Grounded in solid faith in Christ.
_____ c.   Surface-level and short-lived.
_____ d.   Long-distance.

> "May I continue to find favor in your eyes, my lord," she said. "You have given me comfort and have spoken kindly to your servant—though I do not have the standing of one of your servant girls." (Ruth 2:13)

Ruth is a **wise** woman! She doesn't let the attention from Boaz go to her head. She doesn't suddenly start thinking, *I'm all that! The big guy's got it for me.* She keeps her *perspective* and is mindful of her boundaries. She still knows that she's the worker and Boaz is the landowner.

Teen girls often overstep their boundaries at the first sign of interest from a guy. The wise young lady will surrender her dating life to God.

What are the advantages of allowing God to be in charge of your dating life?

Have you made the commitment to put God in charge of your dating relationships? If not, do so right now.

BITE #5

> At mealtime Boaz said to her, "Come over here. Have some bread and dip it in the wine vinegar." When she sat down with the harvesters, he offered her some roasted grain. She ate all she wanted and had some left over. (Ruth 2:14)

Notice what Boaz is offering Ruth—bread and wine vinegar—a picture of communion.

Jesus invites **you** to have daily communion with him. He wants you to experience spiritual intimacy with him as he provides for you.

Identify anything in your life that's keeping you from experiencing spiritual intimacy with God.

How often do you commune/fellowship with God?

Not only does Ruth get full, but she also has leftovers! What does this tell you about the kind of life God wants to give you?

_____ a.   God wants me to eat grain.
_____ b.   God not only wants to be my provider but also to give me a full life!
_____ c.   God wants me to have dinner with a landowner.
_____ d.   God wants me to eat all my meals at restaurants.

Let's take a peek at John 10:10:

> I have come that they may have life, and have it to the full.

According to the above passage, what kind of life does God want you to experience?

Are you living abundantly in Jesus?

List some ways you can have a more abundant spiritual life.

As she got up to glean, Boaz gave orders to his men, "Even if she gathers among the sheaves, don't embarrass her. Rather, pull out some stalks for her from the bundles and leave them for her to pick up, and don't rebuke her." (Ruth 2:15-16)

In other words Boaz tells his workers to leave some of the **best** grain right in Ruth's path so it will be easy for her to collect. If we compare this with our Christian walk, we can use this as a reminder that Christianity doesn't always have to be difficult.

Many people complain about what they've given up to follow Christ. But whatever we surrender to him is nothing in comparison to his sacrifice for us. He gave his life! Salvation is really quite easy. It's a free gift to all who will believe, accept Christ's forgiveness, and live for him.

Ruth still has to put forth an effort to get the grain, but she doesn't have to struggle to find it. When we ask Christ to be Lord of our lives, we receive his forgiveness for free, but we still need to put forth an effort to live in obedience to him.

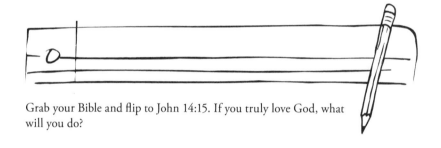

Grab your Bible and flip to John 14:15. If you truly love God, what will you do?

Now read John 14:23. What good things will those who obey God experience?

Now look at John 14:24. What does Christ say about the one who doesn't obey him?

Read John 15:10. Insert your own name into this verse and rewrite it as a letter to yourself from Jesus.

BITE #6

So Ruth gleaned in the field until evening. Then she threshed the barley she had gathered, and it amounted to about an ephah. (Ruth 2:17)

An ephah equals one-half bushel or 22 liters. That's a lot of barley! God uses Boaz to provide abundantly for Ruth.

When has God abundantly provided for you?

Has God worked through any particular person to provide for you? Who?

She carried it back to town, and her mother-in-law saw how much she had gathered. Ruth also brought out and gave her what she had left over after she had eaten enough. Her mother-in-law asked her, "Where did you glean today? Where did you work? Blessed be the man who took notice of you!" (Ruth 2:18-19)

Ruth brings home more than the average worker. It's obvious to Naomi that someone has been kind to Ruth. How have you shown kindness to someone less fortunate than you during the past few weeks?

Read Ruth 2:18-19 again and notice Naomi's response to what Ruth brings home. List as many words as you can that describe the variety of emotions Naomi must be feeling.

*   *

*   *

*   *

*   *

Let's look at Ruth 2:18-19 one more time:

> She carried it back to town, and her mother-in-law saw how much she had gathered. Ruth also brought out and gave her what she had left over after she had eaten enough. Her mother-in-law asked her, "Where did you glean today? Where did you work? Blessed be the man who took notice of you!"

Ruth doesn't haphazardly glean in a scrawny field. She works steadily and gleans in the *lush* field of Boaz. When seeking a place to find food, she headed toward the *best field* she could find. She gleans right where God wants her to glean. What about *your* gleaning habits? Answer the following questions to help determine if you're "gleaning" as you should.

* When you're seeking spiritual nourishment, do you do so half-heartedly or with 100-percent effort?

* When seeking spiritual food, are you content to be satisfied with anything that looks or sounds good, or do you seek absolute truth?

* Are you more likely to "glean" from the latest movie or the Word of God when you're down and in need of encouragement?

* How and where do you find spiritual nourishment?

* We will eventually become what we glean or absorb. Think about the past two weeks. Have you absorbed more from the news or the Bible?

* Are you currently gleaning where God has directed, or are you gleaning on your own?

> Then Ruth told her mother-in-law about the one at whose place she had been working. "The name of the man I worked with today is Boaz," she said. (Ruth 2:19)

Ruth still doesn't know who Boaz is, but Naomi knows. A romance has started to bloom between the important landowner and the poor foreign widow, but she's still **unaware** of the fact that Boaz is related to her and probably still a bit naive in understanding his feelings toward her.

Though **you** don't see and understand everything, take comfort in the fact that God does! God knows all, sees all, and has a wonderful plan for your life.

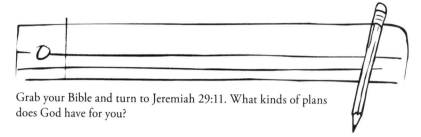

Grab your Bible and turn to Jeremiah 29:11. What kinds of plans does God have for you?

And flip to Ephesians 3:20. According to this passage, how big does God dream for you?

Take a moment to write a letter of gratitude to God for knowing all, loving you more than you can comprehend, and promising to meet your needs. He is your ultimate provider!

BITE #7

"The Lord bless him!" Naomi said to her daughter-in-law. "He has not stopped showing his kindness to the living and the dead." She added, "That man is our close relative; he is one of our kinsman-redeemers." (Ruth 2:20)

Naomi is excited about the fact that Boaz, as their kinsman-redeemer, can *rescue* them from their poverty! As we continue our study, we'll soon see Boaz redeeming Ruth from her dire situation. Jesus Christ was and is our kinsman-redeemer. He redeems us from the bondage of *sin*.

God didn't have to *redeem* us. God wasn't obligated to save us, and we certainly don't deserve to be redeemed. So why did God choose to offer us salvation?

Let's take a peek at one of the most well-known verses in the Bible—John 3:16. According to this passage, what is God's method of redeeming us? (How, what, or whom did God use to offer us salvation?)

Then Ruth the Moabitess said, "He even said to me, 'Stay with my workers until they finish harvesting all my grain.'" Naomi said to Ruth her daughter-in-law, "It will be good for you, my daughter, to go with his girls, because in someone else's field you might be harmed." (Ruth 2:21-22)

Harvest time was a great celebration! Think *party* in the best sense of the word! There would be lots of young men and women present at the harvest celebration. Ruth could easily be swayed to look to a younger man for *romantic* interest. But she's a woman of God and a woman of character. No doubt she feels God's hand on her friendship with Boaz, though she still doesn't have the full picture of what will happen with this *romance*. She's not yet able to see what God has in store for her. But she continues to *trust* God's plan.

Ruth also trusts her mother-in-law. She has watched Naomi live out her faith during the lean years of poverty and grief in Moab. She knows Naomi has a deep, growing, intimate relationship with God.

What do those around you know about your relationship with God? Do you keep it private? Do you talk openly about God? Are you seen as a young woman of faith? Or a young woman of obedience? Or a young woman of uncertainty?

> So Ruth stayed close to the servant girls of Boaz to glean until the barley and wheat harvests were finished. And she lived with her mother-in-law. (Ruth 2:23)

Just as Ruth heeds the advice of her mother-in-law, we too need to heed the advice of older, spiritually mature adults in our lives. Too often we look past an elderly person and his or her advice simply because of age. The truth is many older people in our churches today are saints! They've lived through the lean times and can strongly testify to God's provision. God often chooses to speak through wise adults. If we'd learn to seek them out and listen to them, we'd gain valuable spiritual insights.

Think of an older, spiritually mature person whom you can respect and look to for spiritual guidance. Write his or her name here: _____

Will you jot this person a note of encouragement right now? Let him or her know of your respect and admiration. Ask for prayer from this person and look forward to what God will teach you through this life.

BITE #8

GRAB A FRIEND.

You did it! You just finished the second chapter of Ruth. You're a "secret power" girl, who is growing closer to Christ because you're taking his Word seriously. Now grab a friend and discuss the following questions together.

* Describe what a kinsman-redeemer is.

* Boaz blessed the gleaners in his field. How have I blessed people in my life this past week?

* Boaz affirms Ruth for taking refuge under the wings of God. Was there a time this week when I sought refuge from a person other than God?

* Ruth is a woman of character. How has my character been revealed this week?

MEMORIZE IT!

Try to memorize this verse with your friend and say it to each other the next time you get together.

> "May you be richly rewarded by the LORD, the God of Israel, under whose wings you have come to take refuge." (Ruth 2:12)

MY JOURNAL

Okay, S.P.G., this is your space, so take advantage of it. You can do whatever you want here, but always try to include the following:

* List your prayer requests. (Later, as God answers them, go back and record the date when God answered your prayer.)

* Copy down any verse we studied in the previous chapter that you don't understand. Then let this be a reminder to ask your parents, Sunday school teacher, pastor, or youth leader about it.

* Jot down what stood out the most from this chapter.

Girl Visits Guy

BITE #1

Before we dive into Scripture, let's take a moment to recap. It's been established that *Boaz* is Naomi's relative. Therefore, he's also Ruth's relative. He is her *kinsman-redeemer*. He can save her from her poverty and fill the void in her life that her husband left when he died.

We've looked at a couple of interesting *laws* thus far in the book of Ruth, haven't we? The law that provided food for the poor by allowing them to glean after the harvesters and the kinsman-redeemer law.

To understand the rest of the romance that unfolds in the book of Ruth, we need to take a look at another strange law. It's found in Deuteronomy 25:5-10.

> If brothers are living together and one of them dies without a son, his widow must not marry outside the family. Her husband's brother shall take her and marry her and fulfill the duty of a brother-in-law to her. The first son she bears shall carry on the name of the dead brother so that his name will not be blotted out from Israel.

> However, if a man does not want to marry his brother's wife, she shall go to the elders at the town gate and say, "My husband's brother refuses to carry on his brother's name in Israel. He will not fulfill the duty of a brother-in-law to me." Then the elders of his town shall summon him and talk to him. If he persists in saying, "I do not want to marry her," his brother's widow shall go up to him in the presence of the elders, take off one of his sandals, spit in his face and say, "This is what is done to the man who will not build up his brother's family line." That man's line shall be known in Israel as The Family of the Unsandaled.

While it's tempting to *laugh* at this strange law, it did have a positive spin to it. In those days this law bonded the families *together*. Every family member was extremely interested and involved in the girl each son would marry. *Brothers* were especially interested because they could end up having to marry the woman if their brother died.

As we have seen how the gleaning law was God's *provision* for the poor, we can see two more examples of God's provision in this law as well.

#1: *God wanted to protect women.* Think about it: Back then women without husbands didn't have the legal right to own land. So if a woman's husband died, and she was left with a farm, cattle, sheep, or a vineyard, she'd be up a creek without a paddle—because she had very little legal defense if someone else laid claim to her property. God's law allowed her to claim help immediately through a brother of her husband or the nearest kinsman.

No doubt you've heard many times, "God loves you. God loves everybody." But to know that God's specifically interested in taking care of women should make you feel pretty good! Circle all the words that describe how you feel knowing God has a special interest in you as a young woman.

alone   ticked off   expectant
happy   stubborn   pressured   special
disrespectful   secure   confident
excited   loved   comforted   old
provided for   injured   confused
disobedient   inadequate   pride
respected   cherished

#2: *God wanted to protect land rights.* Earlier in our study of Ruth we learned how God had promised the Israelites land. (It's referred to as The Promised Land.) And not only did God provide land for the nation of Israel, but he also gave each tribe a specific portion of land and each family within the tribe a certain piece of land as well.

But we also learned that a family could lose its land. If you'll flip back to Bite #2 (Chapter Two), you'll recall the example of Mr. Smith. He owns 40 acres of land, but his crops haven't produced, so he sells his land to Mr. Jones (who can only purchase the mortgage for up to 50 years; after that time the land will go back to the Smith family).

Okay, we understand that. It was God's way of keeping the land in the family. But now we see God going a step further to protect land rights. What if a widow married a stranger? He'd have automatic rights to her property. This law (that the widow had to marry within the family of her deceased husband) was God's way of protecting the land for the people.

The Bible makes it extremely clear that God is interested in **every** one of our needs!

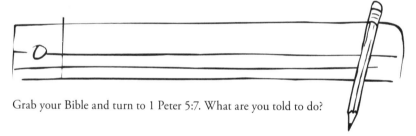

Grab your Bible and turn to 1 Peter 5:7. What are you told to do?

What reason are you given for doing this?

Now turn to Ephesians 5:29. What is Christ's love for the church compared to in this verse?

Check out Psalm 111:5. For whom does God provide food? And how long will God remember this covenant?

Let's look at 1 Timothy 6:17. What does God provide for us?

Take a moment to write a prayer of thanksgiving for God's *provision*. Strive to list specific things God has provided for you. Try not to write a "general" prayer. Really **think** about what you can thank God for!

BITE #2

One day Naomi her mother-in-law said to her, "My daughter, should I not try to find a home for you, where you will be well provided for? Is not Boaz, with whose servant girls you have been, a kinsman of ours?" (Ruth 3:1-2)

Now we come to an interesting twist in this beautiful romance. Ruth knows Boaz is a kinsman-redeemer of hers. He's the one who can step in and provide for her. She knows he's interested in her. He's given quite a few signals. List some of the *signs* Boaz has given Ruth to let her know he's personally interested in her.

*

*

*

*

*

So why doesn't Boaz go ahead and make his move? you may be thinking. *She knows he's interested. Why doesn't he ask her out?*

We're led to believe that he'd *love* to do that right now, but his hands are tied! Boaz has to wait for Ruth to do the claiming! She has to *claim* him as her kinsman-redeemer.

We've discussed how Boaz—as Ruth's kinsman-redeemer—is parallel to Christ being **our** kinsman-redeemer. Now think about another similarity: Just as Ruth has to claim Boaz, you too have to claim Christ as your *Savior*.

Boaz can't force Ruth to claim him. And Jesus won't *force* you to accept him either!

How does this make you feel about Boaz? About God? About Ruth?

Ruth hasn't made her move. So we read that her mother-in-law finally speaks out. Let's take another look at the Scripture:

> One day Naomi her mother-in-law said to her, "My daughter, should I not try to find a home for you, where you will be well provided for? Is not Boaz, with whose servant girls you have been, a kinsman of ours?" (Ruth 3:1-2)

Naomi gently encourages Ruth to move forward. But we need to understand that Naomi isn't being pushy; she's simply nudging Ruth in the direction God wants her to head. We also need to understand that although Ruth is moving forward, she's not being forward. Describe the difference in being forward and moving forward.

Teen girls often make the mistake of taking the initiative in letting a guy know she likes him. *There's nothing wrong with asking a guy out*, she thinks. *And he's so shy! If I don't make a move, nothing will ever happen. So I have to make the first move!*

Whoa! Slow down, girlfriend. We've discussed this before, but it's time for a reminder: It's a **wise** young woman who will allow God to direct her dating relationships. The gal who feels she has to control things herself is a gal who's not allowing God to be in total control of her life.

How can a girl's actions demonstrate that she doesn't fully trust God when she tries to initiate a relationship?

Read the following two scenarios and notice the distinction.

"I've liked Todd forever," Emily tells Beth. "We're good friends, but I wonder if anything will ever develop beyond that."

"Does he know you'd like to become more than friends?" Beth asks.

"I don't know," Emily says.

"Well, maybe you better tell him."

"Ah, I don't know."

"Go ahead, Emily. Just tell him how you feel. You've gotta find out if he likes you back!"

"Okay, Beth. I think I'll write him a note."

"You go, girl!"

"I'm kinda nervous."

"Well…it's a risk to let him know your feelings. But you have to do it, Em! If you don't, you may never know how he feels."

"What if he doesn't feel the same way?"

"You'll never know till you write the note!"

"I just feel kinda weird. I wish he'd just make a move; you know—tell me how he feels—give me a signal, something."

"Yeah, well…not gonna happen," Beth says. "Write the note."

"Okay. I'll do it," Emily says.

"Hi, Emily! How's it going?" Beth asks.

"Whew, I'm tired," Emily says. "Todd and I have been working on our science project for the past two hours."

"You guys sure are good friends, huh?"

Emily laughs. "We really are. We've known each other since kindergarten."

"Wow! That's forever," Beth says. "Have your feelings ever gone beyond friendship?"

"Yeah, I've been crushing on him for the past two years."

"Seriously? Does he know?"

"If he does, he's never said anything."

"And you've never told him?" Beth asks.

"Nope."

"Girl, you gotta let him know! If he knew how you felt, you two might be a serious couple right now," Beth says.

"Yeah, I've thought about that," Emily says. "Todd's everything I want in a guy. He loves the Lord, he's involved in church, and he cares about others. I really like him as more than just a friend."

"Ooooh, girl! This is gettin' good! So write him a note!"

"Nah," Emily says. "I've been praying about it, and I just don't feel it's my place to make my feelings known."

"Okay, what language are *you* talkin'?"

Emily laughs again. "Think about it, Beth. Todd's a smart guy. He's certainly intelligent enough to know that I like him. If he wants to act on that, great! If not, I'll keep being his friend."

"I can't believe this," Beth says. "He's so shy! He's probably scared to say anything—thinking he'll ruin the friendship or something. You've gotta tell him!"

"Not gonna do it. About a year ago, I put my dating life in God's control."

"So? What's that supposed to mean?"

"It means that I believe God is certainly big enough to orchestrate my relationships. If it's God's will for Todd and me to become more than friends, God is powerful enough to make it happen."

"Okay," Beth continues, "but what if you don't see God move? What if Todd *doesn't* say or do anything to place your friendship into the romance category? Then what?"

"Then I keep trusting God. If nothing more than friendship happens between Todd and me, I believe God has someone else in mind for me."

"Yeah, but Em! Don't you wanna know how Todd feels about you?"

"Sure! I'd love to know. But get this, Beth. If I write him a note or talk to him and tell him my feelings for him go deeper than friendship, one of two things will happen: He'll return my feelings and tell me he likes me as more than a friend, too—"

"Yeah! So go for it, Em!"

"Or," Emily continues, "he'll gently let me know that he doesn't feel the same way. That could damage our friendship. Things would be really awkward."

"Love is worth taking the risk. I still say let him know!"

"Hold on, Beth. Even if I tell him my feelings and he returns them, I'll always wonder if he would've ever taken the initiative to make the first move. I've learned I'm valuable in God's eyes, Beth—so valuable that I don't have to take my love life into my own hands. If a guy wants to pursue me, he has to take the first step. I'm worth that."

"Hmmm. I like that," Beth says. "I wanna feel that valuable too. So often I just get ahead of myself and blurt out how I feel. But you know something? I'm worth having a guy approach me too! It shouldn't have to be my responsibility."

"You're exactly right, Beth. And when you totally surrender your dating life to God's control, it takes all the pressure off of you. You don't have to think, *How can I get him to notice me? Does he like me? How can I get his attention?* You can just relax and be friends with the guy and trust that God is big enough to make something more happen if it's God's will."

Do you understand the difference in truly surrendering your relationships to God and in trying to make something happen yourself?

Yeah, but look at Ruth! you may be thinking. *The Bible just said that Naomi told Ruth to make her move.*

Remember the law. In those days a widow had to claim her kinsman-redeemer. Ruth didn't move to Bethlehem and start chasing guys. Her priorities are right. She's focused on God and on taking care of her mother-in-law.

Allowing God to be in charge of your dating life doesn't mean you'll never speak to guys. God wants you to be friendly, reach out, and make those around you comfortable. Guys will naturally gravitate to girls with whom they're comfortable. So learning the art of being a good conversationalist, showing genuine interest in the guy you like, and developing a good friendship are **wise** choices.

But you can do the above without chasing a guy. I believe God created males to be the pursuers. And guess what! You're definitely worth being pursued!

Take a moment to create a pledge allowing God to be in charge of your relationships.

BITE #3

"Tonight he will be winnowing barley on the threshing floor.
Wash and perfume yourself, and put on your best clothes. Then go
down to the threshing floor, but don't let him know you are there
until he has finished eating and drinking. When he lies down,
note the place where he is lying. Then go and uncover his feet and
lie down. He will tell you what to do."

"I will do whatever you say," Ruth answered. (Ruth 3:2-5)

Naomi tells Ruth to get *dressed up*. You can imagine that she uses her best bath
oils and her favorite perfume and puts on the nicest outfit she has. There's nothing
wrong with wanting to *look good*. When we take *care* of ourselves, we usually *feel*
better about ourselves.

Sometimes people think Christians shouldn't be concerned with their **appearance**. Though we're told in Proverbs 31:30 and in 1 Peter 3:3-4 that outer beauty is
fleeting and true beauty comes from the inside, we shouldn't use this as an **excuse**
to let ourselves go. It makes sense to want to look our best, and it only becomes
wrong when we become **obsessed** with our looks.

Ruth does what Naomi tells her. She bathes, dresses, and heads to the threshing
floor. It may **seem** as though Ruth is being forward. But we have to understand the
culture and what the threshing floor was. So pretend you're stepping back in history a few thousand years. Here's the scene: The threshing floor is a smooth *surface*.
It's more than likely clay soil that's been packed and hardened. It's marked off with
rocks in a circular area.

Most threshing floors are at the top of a *hill*, so pretend you're up high. About
midafternoon you begin to feel a *breeze*. The threshing will continue as long as
there's a breeze. If you look closely, you'll notice sheaves of grain all over the floor.
Watch out! Here come the oxen. Don't get in their way. They're *trampling* the
grain that's spread all over the floor.

The oxen aren't the only ones working. The threshing floor is filled with people
wildly *throwing* the grain up into the air. The chaff is blown away by the breeze, and
the *good grain* comes down on the threshing floor.

The threshing won't stop until the *wind* dies down. That might be 5 p.m. or it
could be midnight. At that point you're going to party! Actually it's a religious feast,
a huge *celebration*. After you've had your fill, you'll join the *families* and the rest of

the folks on the threshing floor to catch a few zzzz's. And you're glad because you've worked hard and you're dog tired!

The threshing floor is circular. The men are sleeping with their heads toward the grain, and their feet are sticking out like bicycle spokes. *How come they're sleeping this way?* you may be thinking.

It's to protect the grain from thieves. If someone comes in to steal the grain (he'd have to be pretty brave—or stupid—to try to force his way through all the men lying in the circle), he'll have to walk toward the men to get the grain. Because of the position of each man sleeping, he'll find it easier to jump up and face the thief. In other words the robber has to come toward you; it's impossible for him to sneak around you or creep up behind you.

> So she went down to the threshing floor and did everything her mother-in-law told her to do. (Ruth 3:6)

Ruth doesn't question Naomi because she trusts her mother-in-law's relationship with God. Ruth knows God is leading Naomi in guiding her.

Think of the people in your life who are in authority over you (parents, teachers, youth leader, pastor, etc.). Choose two people and identify what makes it easy for you to trust them.

1.

2.

Do you have difficulty trusting certain people in authority over you? If so, why?

Think about Ruth's past several weeks. She's been gleaning in the field. She's been **taking** grain. Now she's on the threshing floor for a higher purpose.

Now think about yourself for a moment. Maybe you've been gleaning and taking. That's good. We all need to glean; we all need to take and receive. But there comes a point in our spiritual lives when we need to stop taking all the time and start giving.

God has a high calling on your life! And God wants you to glean and take spiritual food—all you can get! But God also wants you to *give*.

During the past two weeks of your life, have you been doing more taking than giving? What have you spiritually **taken,** and what have you spiritually *given?*

> When Boaz had finished eating and drinking and was in good spirits, he went over to lie down at the far end of the grain pile. Ruth approached quietly, uncovered his feet and lay down. In the middle of the night something startled the man, and he turned and discovered a woman lying at his feet. (Ruth 3:7-8)

Let's make sure we're on the *right page* with Ruth. Again she's not being forward *or* improper. Naomi would *never* have suggested that her daughter-in-law do something immoral. The threshing floor is a *public* place. Ruth isn't going to bed with Boaz. She *is* going near him, but it's for a specific *purpose*: to claim him as her kinsman-redeemer.

Ruth is lying at the *feet* of Boaz, and she has pulled the covers away from his feet. The Scripture tells us, "In the middle of the night something startled the man." He may have heard an animal; someone may have thrown an extra log on the fire; or it could have been any number of noises. *But he wakes up.*

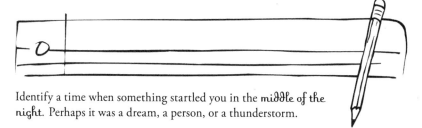

Identify a time when something startled you in the *middle of the night*. Perhaps it was a dream, a person, or a thunderstorm.

When you're afraid, Christ wants you to turn to him. He cares about everything that concerns you! Grab your Bible and turn to Deuteronomy 1:21. What are we told not to do?

Now look at Hebrews 13:6. Who wants to be our helper during scary times?

Read John 14:27. Insert your own name into this verse and rewrite it in your own words in the space provided.

BITE #4

"Who are you?" he asked.

"I am your servant Ruth," she said. "Spread the corner of your garment over me, since you are a kinsman-redeemer." (Ruth 3:9)

Something startles Boaz, and he wakes up. Now that he's awake, he realizes his feet are cold. But when he reaches for the blanket at his feet, he notices a woman. He probably squints his eyes and tries to adjust his sight to the darkness of the night.

Ruth identifies herself.

To identify yourself you have to know who you are. You may feel as though you're right in the middle of ♂iscovering who you really are. It can be a process. Know that true i♂entity is found in a strong, growing, intimate relationship with your creator.

The more you get to know the One who made you,

———— a.   The wealthier you'll become.
———— b.   The more you'll understand who you are.
———— c.   The more you'll enjoy fishing.
———— d.   The more you'll travel.

Besides discovering your own identity, you'll need to discover another identity in life. Every person in the world (you included!) has to decide who ♂esus is. Do you know the identity of Christ? Do you truly understand who he is?

Who **is** Jesus Christ?

———— a.   A good teacher.
———— b.   A prophet.
———— c.   A wise man.
———— d.   The Messiah, Son of God, King of Kings.

John the Baptist, the cousin of Jesus, asked about Christ's identity. Check out Matthew 11:2-3. What does John send his disciples to ask Jesus?

And according to Matthew 11:4-6, what is Jesus' response?

Jesus won't *force* you to believe that he's the Son of God. But for *all* who believe, he forgives sins and grants eternal life! Describe the time when you accepted Jesus Christ as the Son of God and asked him to become your *Savior*.

Back to Ruth. When she went to the threshing floor, where did she lie?

_____ a.   On a waterbed.
_____ b.   On a hammock.
_____ c.   On a tanning bed.
_____ d.   At the feet of Boaz.

Thus far in our study of Ruth, we've seen some parallels between Boaz and Christ. Circle all the similarities.

Jesus & Boaz both had disciples.

Jesus & Boaz never forced people to love them.

Boaz & Jesus provided for the poor.

Boaz & Jesus both loved grain sandwiches.

Jesus & Boaz were kind to all.

Boaz & Jesus ate a unique grain cereal for breakfast every morning of their lives.

Jesus & Boaz both wore Doc Martens sandals.

Boaz is Ruth's kinsman-redeemer, and Christ is our kinsman-redeemer.

Ruth lies at the *feet* of Boaz. Let's take a quick peek at the *feet* of Jesus. He's ruler of the *calm* as he walks on the seashore. He's Lord of the *storm* as he walks on the water's waves. Imagine his *feet* being nailed to the cross for you. These are the same *feet* that left the glory and splendor of heaven to invade your world with *love*. These *feet* were born in a crude, dirty stable. Yet these same feet *walked* to the tomb of Lazarus and raised him from the dead. These are the feet that walked in the *temple* and the feet that walked up Mount Calvary for **you.**

According to John 1:36, what does John the Baptist say when he sees Jesus walking?

Where have the feet of Jesus led you this week as you've walked with him?

BITE #5

Before we dive into further Scripture, let's review a few past verses:

When Boaz had finished eating and drinking and was in good spirits, he went over to lie down at the far end of the grain pile. Ruth approached quietly, uncovered his feet and lay down. In the middle of the night something startled the man, and he turned and discovered a woman lying at his feet.

"Who are you?" he asked. "I am your servant, Ruth," she said. "Spread the corner of your garment over me, since you are a kinsman-redeemer." (Ruth 3:7-9)

Remember that Ruth isn't doing something immoral or immodest in lying at the feet of Boaz. Her actions show Boaz that she wants him to be a spiritual covering for her. She's asking him to become her kinsman-redeemer.

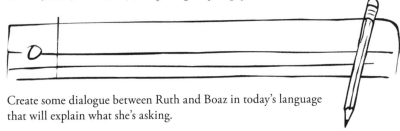

Create some dialogue between Ruth and Boaz in today's language that will explain what she's asking.

Ruth sees Boaz as her only *hope*. As far as she knows, he's her only kinsman-redeemer. He's the only one who can step in and save her, help her, and *provide* for her. Identify a time in your life when your back was against a wall and you realized that *Jesus* was your only hope.

The question now is: *Will Boaz do it?* Will this well-to-do rich man stretch his garment to cover a **poor** Moabite woman who has no money and nothing to offer? Will he do it?

Maybe you're at the *same* point in life. Perhaps you're wondering if God's blanket of forgiveness can actually reach *you*. Can it truly cover *all* your sins? Not only can God's *forgiveness* cover all your sins, but God's *grace* also completely erases your sins!

Grab your *Bible* and turn to Psalm 103:11. According to this passage, how much does God love you?

Now read Psalm 103:12. How *far* have your sins been removed from God's mind?

Imagine! God *chooses* to forget your sins! When you ask Jesus for forgiveness, he completely wipes your record *clean*! You're brand-new…*without stain*. How does this make you feel? (Mark all that apply.)

_____ a. Like jumping up and down on a trampoline forever!
_____ b. Giggly, gracious, giddy, grateful!
_____ c. Like I wanna run into Jesus' arms and thank him for about 10,000 years without stopping!
_____ d. Peaceful, pure, purposeful, polished, pleased, positive!
_____ e. Like drinking a tall, cold glass of lemonade and letting it spill down my chin!
_____ f. Hugs, hallelujah, hopeful, hosanna!
_____ g. Like I wanna live my whole life for Christ in thanks for what He's done for me!
_____ h. Forgiven, fanciful, free!
_____ i. _____

Christ is your *redeemer*! This is a word that indicates a *continued* state of action. In other words Christ didn't simply redeem you one time when you gave your life to him and that was it. He will continually, *consistently*, constantly cover you with his garment, forgive you, and provide for you no matter how long you've lived in Moab—the garbage dump.

God will always forgive a *repentant* heart. God will continue to redeem *genuine* confession. But genuine repentance doesn't say, "Tonight I'll ask God to forgive me for shoplifting this lipstick. But tomorrow if I don't have enough money to buy that CD I want, I'll probably just grab it and ask God to forgive me later. Then next week I may go shopping and take a pair of jeans. I'll just ask God to forgive me again. And when it's time for prom, I'll probably lift some new shoes. God will forgive me."

That's **not** genuine repentance!

Genuine repentance says, "Oh, dear Lord. I'm so sorry I sinned. Will you forgive me? I realize that by sinning, I've broken your heart. I'm so sorry. I don't ever plan on going that direction again. In fact I'm going to set up some accountability and safeguards in my life that will help me stay away from this area of sin. I'm so sorry."

As we studied in our *Secret Power* book on 1 *Peter*, when we've totally surrendered every area in our life to Christ, and when we yield to the authority of his Holy Spirit in our lives, we don't have to continue living as *slaves* to sin. God wants to *free* us from being enslaved to sin.

Look at what the apostle John says in 1 John 2:1.

> **My dear children, I write this to you so that you will not sin.**

John wouldn't have told us not to sin if it weren't *possible*! We're not puppets! We don't have to be *controlled* by our sinful desires. With God's Holy Spirit ruling, *empowering,* and saturating our lives, we *can* say no to temptation!

But we're still human. There may be times when we don't say no, and we *do* sin. If that happens, what will we do? We can find the answer in 1 John 2:1:

> **But if anybody does sin, we have one who speaks to the Father in our defense—Jesus Christ, the Righteous One.**

That's proof that God will always forgive a genuinely repentant heart! Christ will *continue to redeem* us when we come to him and offer confession.

Take a moment and ask God if there is any unconfessed sin in your life right now for which you need to seek forgiveness. Use Psalm 139:23-24 as your prayer guide.

BITE #6

> "The LORD bless you, my daughter," he replied. "This kindness is greater than that which you showed earlier: You have not run after the younger men, whether rich or poor." (Ruth 3:10)

We quickly realize from this passage that Boaz is willing to be Ruth's kinsman-redeemer. He has been impressed with Ruth. He's watched her and admired her lifestyle. It's as if he's saying, "I noticed you didn't move here and simply start chasing guys. You focused entirely on God. You're not flippant. You haven't let the young, good-looking guys distract you. You've kept your focus. I like that. You have tons of character. You're trustworthy."

> "And now, my daughter, don't be afraid. I will do for you all you ask. All my fellow townsmen know that you are a woman of noble character." (Ruth 3:11)

Yes! Boaz is not only *willing* to be her kinsman-redeemer—but he also *wants* to be her kinsman-redeemer. He's been anxiously waiting for her to claim him.

Again how does this parallel with Christ wanting to be your redeemer?

Let's take another look at Boaz's last sentence in this passage:

> "All my fellow townsmen know that you are a woman of noble character." (Ruth 3:11)

Ruth's reputation has gotten around town. Everyone knows she's a woman of integrity. They admire her. What would your fellow townsmen say about you? Finish this sentence about yourself: "All the other students know that you are a woman of _____."

Let's take another look at Ruth 3:10:

> "The Lord bless you, my daughter," he replied. "This kindness is greater than that which you showed earlier: You have not run after the younger men, whether rich or poor."

The fact that Ruth has chosen to glean in the field of Boaz

_____ a. Ticks him off.
_____ b. Makes him laugh.
_____ c. Makes him happy.
_____ d. Confuses him.

Boaz takes it as a compliment that Ruth has selected his field instead of another. Can you imagine how happy Jesus is and was when you chose him to be your Savior? Try to imagine your redeemer saying this to you:

"I know there are tons of *religions* talked about today. But I'm so happy you've chosen *Christianity*. It's the only true faith! I am the absolute *only* way you'll ever get to heaven. And you've made the right choice! I'm so *glad* you're serving the one true God!"

Do you know that when you make wise choices, when you give God praise, and when you focus on God, you're actually *blessing* God?

Imagine your redeemer saying this to you:

"You have lots of choices on Sunday morning, but you've chosen to be in my house with my people. That blesses me. You had other options: You could have slept in, gone shopping, or watched TV. But you're where you need to be, and you're lifting your voice in praise to me—I'm blessed by that."

Create what you can imagine your redeemer saying to you as you read, study, and memorize Scripture.

Boaz is not only willing, but he's also excited to be Ruth's kinsman-redeemer. The love story is unfolding, isn't it? How do you view your relationship with your Savior? (Mark all that apply.)

I don't know.

I don't have a relationship with him. Jesus is not only my savior, but he's also my best friend.

I delight in my relationship with Christ.

My relationship with Christ is based on fear. It's a love relationship. It's an obligation.

I have a lot of doubts. I'm so happy I'm serving Jesus.

Christ **passionately** loves you. He willingly *died* for you! One of the most exciting things about Christianity is that we can enjoy a warm, loving, personal relationship with the Creator of the universe! How has your lifestyle reflected this in the past week?

BITE #7

"Although it is true that I am near of kin, there is a kinsman-redeemer nearer than I. Stay here for the night, and in the morning if he wants to redeem, good; let him redeem. But if he is not willing, as surely as the Lord lives I will do it. Lie here until morning." (Ruth 3:12-13)

What?! Now we find out that Boaz actually isn't the closest living relative to Naomi and Ruth. How does Boaz know that? We can assume that he's so anxious to become Ruth's kinsman-redeemer that he's **checked** around to see if he actually is the next in line. But in his search, he discovered that there's another man who actually is more closely related to her than himself.

Boaz doesn't send Ruth home. He **protects** her by not letting her out on the dark streets of Bethlehem at night. He's **concerned** for her safety. Your redeemer also wants to protect and comfort **you**.

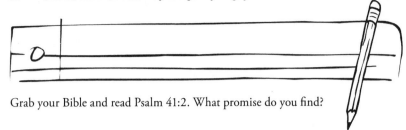

Grab your Bible and read Psalm 41:2. What promise do you find?

Check out Psalm 91:14. Why will God protect you?

Look at 2 Corinthians 1:3-4. Who will comfort you in all your troubles?

Why will God comfort you?

According to Jeremiah 31:13, what does God want to give you?

Boaz also comforts Ruth by telling her: *Lie down; go to sleep; don't worry about it; I'll take care of things.* When you're faced with uncertainty, Jesus wants you to trust him and let him take care of your problems. Let's look at Proverbs 3:5-6:

> Trust in the Lord with all your heart and lean not on your own understanding; in all your ways acknowledge him, and he will make your paths straight.

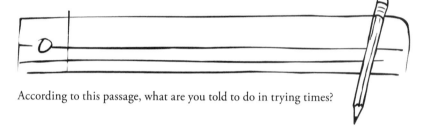

According to this passage, what are you told to do in trying times?

And what benefit will you reap if you trust God?

Grab your Bible and flip to Proverbs 22:19. Whom should you trust?

Now flip to Isaiah 8:17. What two things are you encouraged to do?

Take a peek at Isaiah 12:2:

> Surely God is my salvation; I will trust and not be afraid. The LORD, the LORD, is my strength and my song; he has become my salvation.

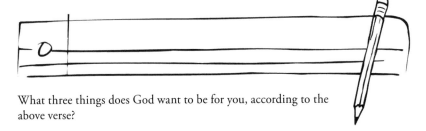

What three things does God want to be for you, according to the above verse?

1.

2.

3.

What does God tell you to do instead of being afraid?

Now turn to Isaiah 26:4. How long should you trust in the Lord?

What is the Lord compared to in this passage?

In what areas of your life do you have the most difficulty trusting God?

Write out a prayer, placing these areas in God's care.

BITE #8

> So she lay at his feet until morning, but got up before anyone
> could be recognized; and he said, "Don't let it be known that a
> woman came to the threshing floor." (Ruth 3:14)

Boaz knows another man is more closely related to Ruth and Naomi. He wants
Ruth to leave the threshing floor before anyone else can see her, in case the other
relative has any interest in her. If the other man is interested in becoming Ruth's
kinsman-redeemer and knows Boaz is also interested, he may quickly exclude Boaz.
Boaz wants to handle this himself.

> He also said, "Bring me the shawl you are wearing and hold it
> out." When she did so, he poured into it six measures of barley
> and put it on her. Then he went back to town. (Ruth 3:15)

Boaz gives Ruth an extremely generous gift, doesn't he? How many measures of
barley does he give her? _____

This is interesting. We're told in Genesis that God created the world in six
days. God worked for six and rested on the seventh after the work was complete.

Perhaps Boaz is sending a message to Naomi through Ruth. "Don't worry, I'll
work at this. I'll work hard at it, and I won't rest until my work is completed—until
Ruth is my wife."

If this is a message from Boaz, it goes right over Ruth's head. But remember,
she's still a young believer. Her faith is still growing. She hasn't walked with the
Lord as long as her mother-in-law has.

But even if Ruth doesn't get the tricky message, we're led to believe in verse 18
that Naomi understands.

> When Ruth came to her mother-in-law, Naomi asked, "How did it
> go, my daughter?"
>
> Then she told her everything Boaz had done for her and added,
> "He gave me these six measures of barley, saying, 'Don't go back
> to your mother-in-law empty-handed.'"
>
> Then Naomi said, "Wait, my daughter, until you find out what
> happens. For the man will not rest until the matter is settled
> today." (Ruth 3:16-18)

In other words, "Ruth, you can relax now. Sit back and wait. Boaz will work it all out. In fact, he's a man on a mission! He won't even stop to rest until he's accomplished his goal."

Your purpose as a young woman is *not* to go out and make something happen with a guy. *Wait*. Let God and the guy work it out!

In what areas of your life do you find it most difficult to wait on God's timing?

Ruth rests. She's done all she can do. She's claimed Boaz as her redeemer; now he'll do the rest.

When we come to Christ, we come in faith. All he asks is that we confess our sins, accept his gift of forgiveness, and live for him. He *doesn't* ask us to pay for our sins. He *doesn't* suggest that we try to "work it all out" or earn our salvation. *We can't*. We just have to surrender, rest, and let him do his wonderful work within us.

And the exciting part? He's given us a *promise* concerning the work that he's doing inside us. Read Philippians 1:6 and jot down what is said about the work God is doing inside *you*.

BITE #9

GRAB A FRIEND.

Yahoo! You just finished the third chapter of Ruth. Now grab a friend and discuss the following questions together.

* Am I demonstrating that God is in control of my dating life and that I fully trust God? Or have I taken control and tried to make things happen with a guy this week?

* Is there anything in my lifestyle that's immodest in my relationship with guys? (examples: the way I dress, the way I act, etc.)

* How have I blessed God this week?

* Describe a specific time this week that you turned to God for comfort and protection during uncertain times.

MEMORIZE IT!

Try to memorize this verse with your friend and say it to each other the next time you get together.

> All my fellow townsmen know that you are a woman of noble character. (Ruth 3:11)

MY JOURNAL

Okay, S.P.G., this is your space, so take advantage of it. You can do whatever you want here, but always try to include the following:

* ✳ List your prayer requests. (Later, as God answers them, go back and record the date when God answered your prayer.)

* ✳ Copy down any verse we studied in the previous chapter that you don't understand. Then let this be a reminder to ask your parents, Sunday school teacher, pastor, or youth leader about it.

* ✳ Jot down what stood out the most from this chapter.

Girl Gets Guy

BITE #1

Meanwhile Boaz went up to the town gate and sat there. (Ruth 4:1)

Where does Boaz go?

———— a. He goes to the courthouse.
———— b. He goes to the city gate.
———— c. He goes to the place where business transactions occur.

Boaz actually goes to all of the above. The town gate served as sort of a courthouse in those days. It was the place where all business transactions happened.

Why does Boaz go to the town gate?

———— a. He wants to climb over the gate and escape.
———— b. He wants to take the other kinsman to court.
———— c. He knows the kinsman would have to enter through the gate at some time during the day.
———— d. He's planning on killing the other relative at the courthouse.

Boaz knows that the other relative will **eventually** have to walk through the gate, so he **waits** there for him. Boaz wants to act quickly and make himself Ruth's legal kinsman-redeemer, so he will meet the man at the gate and take him to court.

Boaz is certainly going out of his way for *Ruth*, isn't he? Describe how *Christ* went out of his way for you.

Identify a time when **you** went out of your way for someone you loved.

> When the kinsman-redeemer he had mentioned came along, Boaz said, "Come over here, my friend, and sit down." So he went over and sat down. (Ruth 4:1)

We don't know the exact *relation* of this other man to Naomi. In those days you were a relative or you weren't. People weren't referred to as a *second cousin* or a cousin once-removed. You were related or you weren't.

This other man may be a *brother* of Naomi's deceased husband, Elimelech. Perhaps Boaz is simply a *cousin*. They probably know each other because they're related and both lived and worked in *Bethlehem*.

Take a moment to list a few of your favorite relatives and how they're related to you.

Name	Relation to You
1.	
2.	
3.	
4.	

> Boaz took ten of the elders of the town and said, "Sit here," and they did so. (Ruth 4:2)

These elders act as judges. Boaz is doing everything by the book. He knows the law and he's abiding by it. Describe a time when you tried to skirt around the law (an actual law of the land, a household rule, a school policy, a rule of church camp or youth retreat, etc.), but it didn't work.

Most laws and rules were created for our protection. Of course there are a few unjust laws, such as those that prohibit Christians in certain countries from proclaiming their faith. Can you think of any other unjust laws?

Think about a few of the laws of our land. List three laws that serve to protect you.

1.

2.

3.

It's always wise to obey God's laws. Check out Psalm 119:24. How does David (the psalmist) feel about God's laws (or statutes)?

Now take a peek at Psalm 119:33-34:

> Teach me, O LORD, to follow your decrees; then I will keep them to the end. Give me understanding, and I will keep your law and obey it with all my heart.

What does David want to learn?

What is he committed to doing after he learns this?

Look at Psalm 119:54:

> Your decrees are the theme of my song wherever I lodge.

David loves God's laws (decrees) so much that he sings about them. Why do you suppose he loves God's laws?

_____ a.   He doesn't want to go to jail.

_____ b.   He knows if he could please God by following the laws, they would also keep him out of trouble.

_____ c.   He was running for mayor and had to memorize all the laws.

_____ d.   He wanted to impress those around him who were in the police force.

What benefits will **you** experience from following God's laws (commands, decrees, ways)?

BITE #2

> Then he said to the kinsman-redeemer, "Naomi, who has come back from Moab, is selling the piece of land that belonged to our brother Elimelech. I thought I should bring the matter to your attention and suggest that you buy it in the presence of these seated here and in the presence of the elders of my people. If you will redeem it, do so. But if you will not, tell me, so I will know. For no one has the right to do it except you, and I am next in line." (Ruth 4:3-4)

It may seem as though Boaz is acting flippant about becoming Ruth's kinsman-redeemer. It sounds as though he doesn't care if this other man claims his right. But Boaz actually has a keen strategy in mind. Things aren't as they seem!

There will be several times in your life when you won't understand the ways of God. God never asks you to understand; God simply wants you to obey.

Our minds are limited and human. We have a hard time understanding God's logic. Match the following.

1. The last shall be _____.   a.   last
   (Luke 13:30)
2. To be great, you must be a _____.   b.   weak
   (Matthew 20:26)
3. Whoever loses his life will _____ it.   c.   servant
   (Matthew 10:39)
4. The first shall be _____.   d.   first
   (Luke 13:30)
5. The strong will be made _____.   e.   find
   (1 Corinthians 1:27)

(You can find the correct answers at the end of Bite #2.)

Grab your Bible and turn to John 14:21. According to this Scripture, what will you do if you love God?

And what benefit will you reap?

You don't have to understand God's ways to obey God. Look at what's in Isaiah 55:8.

> "For my thoughts are not your thoughts, neither are your ways my ways," declares the Lord.

We may never fully understand God's ways until we get to heaven. Let's continue in Isaiah. Read 55:9. What are God's ways and thoughts higher than?

Again we may not always understand God's ways, but with God's help we can learn to trust and accept without understanding! Take a moment right now to ask God for faith and spiritual maturity to accept God's ways without having to understand them.

(Answers to the quiz on p. 102: 1. first 2. servant 3. find 4. last 5. weak)

BITE #3

At first glance in the Scripture, we don't understand the ways of Boaz. We have to continue reading to see his strategy.

Thus far Boaz hasn't even mentioned Ruth, though she's the main focus of his interest. He's only brought up the fact that Naomi has land. The law stated that property had to be redeemed before a person could be redeemed.

"I will redeem it," he said. (Ruth 4:4)

Obviously Naomi's relative is trying to do the right thing. He must have been a generous man to want to purchase the land and give it back to Naomi so she wouldn't have to wait until the Year of Jubilee. He can be commended for that.

Boaz probably had a knot the size of a mountain in his stomach when he heard those words. But he'd also thought ahead. He knew this was a possibility. So he presents the rest of the scenario.

> Then Boaz said, "On the day you buy the land from Naomi and from Ruth the Moabitess, you acquire the dead man's widow, in order to maintain the name of the dead with his property." (Ruth 4:5)

Uh-oh. Trouble for the relative. He didn't know there will be a marriage if he claims the land. But now he realizes that to redeem the land, he'll also have to marry Ruth.

Notice how Boaz describes Ruth: "the Moabitess." Grab your Bible and turn to Deuteronomy 23:3. Who was not allowed into the congregation of the Lord?

According to the law, if this relative brings Ruth into the assembly of the Lord, he'll be jeopardizing his own property. That's a big chance to take.

Boaz doesn't think twice about taking such a risk. He is in love with Ruth. He's willing to do whatever it takes to redeem her—at any cost!

How does this compare with Christ's love for you and the price he paid for your soul?

> At this, the kinsman-redeemer said, "Then I cannot redeem it because I might endanger my own estate. You redeem it yourself. I cannot do it." (Ruth 4:6)

The man may already have a family. But even if he jeopardizes his own *property*, can you imagine how happy Boaz must feel? At this moment he knows he will get to be Ruth's *kinsman-redeemer*!

Christ tells us that all of *heaven* breaks out in a giant party when someone gives his or her life to the Lord. The angels, the saints—everyone *celebrates* big time! Nothing makes God *happier* than for people to surrender to him.

God will probably have a "welcome home" party for you when you arrive in *heaven*. Describe what you *imagine* that may be like.

BITE #4

> Now in earlier times in Israel, for the redemption and transfer of property to become final, one party took off his sandal and gave it to the other. This was the method of legalizing transactions in Israel. So the kinsman-redeemer said to Boaz, "Buy it yourself." And he removed his sandal. (Ruth 4:7-8)

You might remember from earlier in our study, the *law* stated that if a kinsman-redeemer refused to help out his relative, the woman could *spit* on him and remove his sandal. Boaz doesn't spit on the guy, but he *does* remove his sandal. He's acting in Ruth's place. Technically, *she* should be there. She should be the one to go through all the legalities and details. But Boaz wants to take care of things *for* her. He takes her place.

Describe how Jesus has taken your place.

Someday you'll stand before God for judgment. Because Christ will stand in front of you, the Father will see his perfect Son instead of your humanness. Imagine this conversation:

> Father: "Why should I let her into my perfect kingdom? She has sinned."
>
> Son (stepping in front of you): "Yes, Father, she has sinned. But I chose to pay the price for her. Because I died, my blood has erased her sin. She is cleansed. Her sin is no more."
>
> Father: "Yes, My Son. When I look at her, I actually see you. Let her into my kingdom. We'll celebrate our love for her!"

What are your reactions to the above scenario?

Boaz stands in the gap for Ruth. Grab your Bible and turn to Ezekiel 22:30. For whom is God looking?

Where does God want him to stand?

Notice God doesn't say, "I'm looking for the smartest person in your state to stand in the gap. I'm searching for the most popular girl. I'm hoping to find the best athlete in your school to stand in the gap. I'm only looking for the most qualified."

Jesus didn't say that, did he? He's looking for anyone! Anyone who's simply available will do! Are you totally available to Christ?

_____ a.   I'm available most Sundays.
_____ b.   Yes, I'm available. I'll do anything he asks me.
_____ c.   I'm available for a price.
_____ d.   I'm available if my friends are.

God wants your availability. All through Scripture it's obvious God doesn't always choose people with ability. God always chose people with *availability*!

God doesn't always choose the qualified; he qualifies those he chooses. Don't be afraid of what you can't do for God. If you're simply available, God will take care of the rest.

Ruth, in faith, claims Boaz as her kinsman-redeemer. He takes care of everything else. Jesus can do mighty things through the person who's totally available to him!

In which areas of your life do you find it most difficult to be available for God?

Write a letter to Christ that either asks him to help you become totally available to him or pledges your total availability to him.

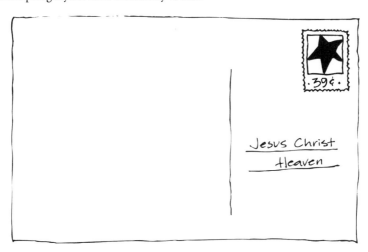

BITE #5

Then Boaz announced to the elders and all the people, "Today you are witnesses that I have bought from Naomi all the property of Elimelech, Kilion and Mahlon. I have also acquired Ruth the Moabitess, Mahlon's widow, as my wife, in order to maintain the name of the dead with his property, so that his name will not disappear from among his family or from the town records. Today you are witnesses!" (Ruth 4:9-10)

First Boaz redeems the *property;* then he redeems *Ruth.* He does this because he *wants to. He's in love with her!*

Christ didn't die for you because he had to. He *willingly* went to the cross because he loved his *Father* and wanted to do his will and also because he loved (and continues to love) *you!*

When you think about it, Christianity is really

———— a.   A big fairy tale.
———— b.   Available only to athletes.
———— c.   A wonderful love story.
———— d.   Possible only if you live in Texas.

Have you ever thought of Christianity as a love story? Christ has *pursued* you with a passion since the day you were created! How does this make you feel?

> Then the elders and all those at the gate said, "We are witnesses. May the LORD make the woman who is coming into your home like Rachel and Leah, who together built up the house of Israel. May you have standing in Ephrathah and be famous in Bethlehem. Through the offspring the LORD gives you by this young woman, may your family be like that of Perez, whom Tamar bore to Judah." (Ruth 4:11-12)

It sounds as though the elders (judges) are

_____ a.   Really angry.
_____ b.   Really crazy.
_____ c.   Really mean.
_____ d.   Really happy.

The elders are *rejoicing*! They're happy that a foreigner *left* her pagan gods and put her faith in the one true God. They know she's made a *sacrifice* to trust the Lord. They realize she didn't come to Bethlehem to chase guys. *Her priorities are right.* She's obviously a woman of good character and willing to work hard to provide for herself and her mother-in-law. And through it all, she hasn't become *bitter* or longed for her old life. *She's consistent.*

What have you left behind to follow God? (attitudes, friendships, relationships, habits, etc.)

Name at least three people who rejoice with you in your faith.

1.

2.

3.

BITE #6

Throughout Scripture Christ refers to the church as his

———— a.   Sore spot.
———— b.   Bride.
———— c.   Joke.
———— d.   Thorn in the flesh.

Boaz takes Ruth as his *bride*. Christ also receives **you** as his bride. To become his bride, what kind of **covenant** is necessary?

Take a moment to write out your wedding vows to Christ as you pledge to be his bride forever.

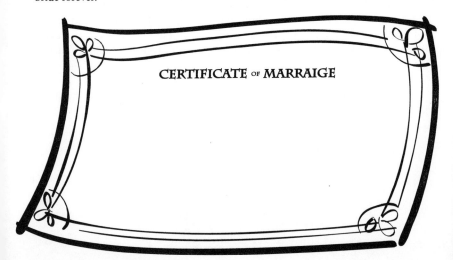

CERTIFICATE OF MARRAIGE

> So Boaz took Ruth and she became his wife. Then he went to her, and the Lord enabled her to conceive, and she gave birth to a son. The women said to Naomi, "Praise be to the Lord, who this day has not left you without a kinsman-redeemer. May he become famous throughout Israel! He will renew your life and sustain you in your old age. For your daughter-in-law, who loves you and who is better to you than seven sons, has given him birth." (Ruth 4:13-15)

Naomi needs a kinsman to carry on the line of her deceased husband, Elimelech. Ruth needs a kinsman to provide for her. You need a kinsman to redeem you. But there are millions of others living without hope, without purpose; they too, need a kinsman-redeemer. Name three people you know who need to be redeemed.

1.

2.

3.

Take a moment right now to pray for each of the people on your list. Ask Christ to reveal how you can make them aware that he wants to redeem them.

> Then Naomi took the child, laid him in her lap and cared for him. The women living there said, "Naomi has a son." And they named him Obed. He was the father of Jesse, the father of David.
>
> This, then, is the family line of Perez:
> Perez was the father of Hezron,
> Hezron the father of Ram,
> Ram the father of Amminadab,
> Amminadab the father of Nahshon,
> Nahshon the father of Salmon,
> Salmon the father of Boaz,
> Boaz the father of Obed,
> Obed the father of Jesse,
> and Jesse the father of David.
>
> (Ruth 4:16-22)

We learn that Ruth later gives birth to a son. This is Naomi's grandson. She rejoices in him and lays him in her lap. She probably loves being a grandma! What a journey Naomi has experienced. She has gone from a great family living in the city of bread and the house of praise to the garbage dump.

While in the dump, she grieved the death of her husband and two sons. When she returned to the city of bread, she only returned with **one** daughter-in-law. Her land wasn't even her own anymore. But God provided for her. God redeemed!

And what a journey Ruth has had. She had to face the death of her husband before she'd been able to give birth. She left all that was familiar and placed her faith in a God she couldn't see. She trusted the God of her mother-in-law and moved to Bethlehem.

She did backbreaking labor and gained the attention of a wealthy landowner who admired her faith in God and her priorities. God redeemed her through Boaz. God blessed them with children, and eventually the King of Kings—Jesus Christ—would be born of this lineage!

Jesus has the power to make good things come from seemingly hopeless situations. He has the desire to redeem us from our sins and continue a good work in us.

What in your life has been less than desirable but God has turned into something beautiful or valuable?

BITE #7

GRAB A FRIEND.

Major applause for you! You just completed the entire book of Ruth! Now grab a friend and discuss the following questions together.

✳ I don't always understand God's ways, but I want to learn to accept them without understanding. I realize this takes spiritual maturity and faith. Has there been a situation this week in which I demonstrated (or should have demonstrated) spiritual maturity and faith even though I didn't fully understand?

✳ Was there a time this past week when I should have been more observant of the law (or rules) around me? Or was there a time I did what was right according to the law (or rules) though I may not have agreed with them?

✳ Who are some relatives I need to connect with? Remind them I love them? Send a note to? Encourage?

✳ How have I demonstrated my love for Jesus by obeying him?

MEMORIZE IT!

Try to memorize this verse with your friend and say it to each other the next time you get together.

"He will renew your life and sustain you in your old age." (Ruth 4:15)

MY JOURNAL

Okay, S.P.G., this is your space, so take advantage of it. You can do whatever you want here, but always try to include the following:

* List your prayer requests. (Later, as God answers them, go back and record the date when God answered your prayer.)

* Copy down any verse we studied in the previous chapter that you don't understand. Then let this be a reminder to ask your parents, Sunday school teacher, pastor, or youth leader about it.

* Jot down what stood out the most from this chapter.

P.S.: (in your journal) The **title** of this book promises you'll deepen your **faith**, learn about **family**, and discover how to get the **guy**. So let's see if you caught it.

Ruth's mother-in-law (family) is so **important** to her that Ruth **listens** to her, **loves** her, and **obeys** her. Which of those three do you find easiest to do with your family?

Which of the three do you find most difficult?

It's God's will that you get along with your **family**. God is the **author of peace** and wants to breed unity in your family. There are two keys to listening to, loving, and obeying your family.

⚷ *Loving God.* Ask God to help you fall more in love with him every single day. As you do, you'll learn to see your family through God's eyes and to hear them through God's ears. If you truly love God, he'll teach you how to love your family.

⚷ *Communication.* Ruth and Naomi have great communication. They openly share with one another. If you'll communicate gently and honestly with your family, listening to, loving, and obeying them will come a lot easier!

Now about **faith**. If you'll stop trying to figure it all out and simply accept Jesus even though you don't have full understanding of his ways, your faith will explode!

Faith isn't about understanding; it's about **believing** even though you *don't* understand. Check this out:

> Now faith is being sure of what we hope for and certain of what we do not see. (Hebrews 11:1)

Ruth demonstrated faith when she left her hometown for an unfamiliar land. She could have prayed this to God: "I doubt I'll get married in Bethlehem. I'll probably be seen as an outcast. I know I'm walking into poverty. But I believe Bethlehem is where you want me. I have placed my faith in you. So even though I can't see what's ahead, I'm going to trust you anyway. I'll follow you all the way, God!"

How can **you** demonstrate this kind of faith with regard to your future?

Do you realize the pressure that's been taken off of you? You don't have to understand and know the future! All you have to do is simply relax and follow God. This should make your faith *shine*!

And about getting the *guy*. Hopefully, you learned that if you trust God with your dating life, you won't have to step in and take the initiative with guys. God created **men** to be the pursuers. So relax, sit back, and *enjoy being pursued* by the right guy in God's perfect timing!

SECRET POWER TO JOY IS ABOUT FINDING THE JOY ONLY GOD CAN GIVE. YOU'LL STUDY THE BOOK OF PHILIPPIANS AND LEARN GREAT STUFF ABOUT HOW THE HOLY SPIRIT HELPS BELIEVERS FIND REAL HAPPINESS DESPITE WHAT'S GOING ON IN THEIR LIVES OR ON THEIR HEADS.

Secret Power to Joy, Becoming a Star, and Great Hair Days
A Personal Bible Study on the Book of Philippians
Susie Shellenberger

RETAIL $9.99
ISBN 0-310-25678-X

THIS BOOK WILL HELP YOU FIGURE OUT WHAT DOES AND DOESN'T FIT WITH BEING A CHRISTIAN. YOU CAN DO THIS STUDY AT YOUR OWN PACE BY YOURSELF, WITH A FRIEND, OR WITH A BUNCH OF FRIENDS.

Secret Power to Treasures, Purity, and a Good Complexion
A Personal Bible Study on the Book of Colossians
Susie Shellenberger

RETAIL $9.99
ISBN 0-310-25679-8

AUTHOR SUSIE SHELLENBERGER LEADS GIRL READERS, AGES 13 TO 17, ON AN ENGAGING EXPLORATION OF 1 PETER. THROUGH HER TRUE-TO-LIFE ANECDOTES AND FUN ASSIGNMENTS, STUDENTS WILL COME TO REALIZE THAT HAPPINESS AND SUCCESS COME BY DRESSING THEMSELVES WITH THE CHAMPIONSHIP ATTIRE THAT'S THEIRS BECAUSE OF WHAT JESUS DID ON THE CROSS.

Secret Power to Winning, Happiness, and a Cool Wardrobe
A Personal Bible Study on the Book of 1 Peter
Susie Shellenberger

RETAIL $9.99
ISBN 0-310-25680-1

invert

Visit www.invertbooks.com or your local bookstore.

WHEN YOU SEE YOUR IMAGE, DO YOU SEE EVERYTHING THAT IS WRONG WITH YOU? HAIR THAT DOESN'T LOOK RIGHT OR A BODY THAT YOU DON'T WANT? *MIRROR MIRROR* IS PACKED WITH RAW HONESTY AND TRUTH, NOT EASY ANSWERS OR PACKAGED SOLUTIONS. IT WILL HELP YOU THINK DEEPER ABOUT BEAUTY, SELF-IMAGE, ACCEPTANCE, HEALTH, SEX, GOD'S LOVE, AND MORE.

Mirror Mirror
Reflections on Who You Are and Who You'll Become
Kara Powell, Kendall Payne

RETAIL $12.99
ISBN 0-310-24886-8

HAVE YOU EVER WONDERED WHY GUYS ACT LIKE COMPLETELY DIFFERENT PEOPLE WHEN THEIR FRIENDS ARE AROUND? OR WHY YOU CAN'T GET THE GUYS IN YOUR LIFE TO TALK ABOUT ANYTHING BESIDES SPORTS? *WHAT'S UP WITH BOYS?* IS THE BOOK FOR YOU! DO THE GUYS IN YOUR LIFE A FAVOR—READ THIS BOOK. THEY'LL LOVE YOU FOR IT.

What's Up with Boys?
Everything You Need to Know about Guys
Crystal Kirgiss

RETAIL $9.99
ISBN 0-310-25489-2

invert

Visit www.invertbooks.com or your local bookstore.

DRAWING ON NINE YEARS OF COUNSELING EXPERIENCE, SCRIPTURE, AND THE LATEST MEDICAL STUDIES, AUTHOR PAM STENZEL GOES BEYOND WARNINGS AND SENTIMENT TO FOCUS ON THE CONSEQUENCES OF PREMARITAL SEX. INCLUDED ARE PERSONAL STUDENT TESTIMONIES, PRACTICAL SOLUTIONS, SUPPORT AND NETWORKING OPTIONS, INNOVATIVE ALTERNATIVES TO DATING SITUATIONS, AND CREATIVE JOURNALING PROMPTS FOR STUDENTS.

Sex Has a Price Tag
Discussions about Sexuality, Spirituality, and Self Respect

Pam Stenzel with Crystal Kirgiss

RETAIL $9.99
ISBN 0-310-24971-6

HAVE YOU EVER WONDERED WHY GUYS ACT LIKE COMPLETELY
DIFFERENT PEOPLE WHEN THEIR FRIENDS ARE AROUND?

OR WHY YOU CAN'T GET THE GUYS IN YOUR LIFE TO TALK
ABOUT ANYTHING BESIDES SPORTS?

WHAT'S UP WITH BOYS? IS FOR YOU! DO THE GUYS IN YOUR
LIFE A FAVOR—READ THIS BOOK.

THEY'LL LOVE YOU FOR IT.

What's Up with Boys?
Everything You Need to Know about Guys

Crystal Kirgiss

RETAIL $9.99
ISBN 0-310-25489-2